THE JEWEL
OF THE
GOLD COAST

Mrs. Potter Palmer's Chicago

SALLY SEXTON KALMBACH

D1715704

AMP&RSAND, INC.

Chicago, Illinois

ISBN 978-098181266-3
Second Edition September 2009

DESIGN
David Robson, Robson Design

PUBLISHED BY
Ampersand, Inc.
1050 North State Street
Chicago, IL 60610
www.ampersandworks.com

Printed in Canada

The typefaces used in this book are New Caledonia,
a modern version of the popular 1890s typeface Scotch Roman,
and Zaner, based on the handwriting styles
of the most influential penman in American history,
Charles Paxton Zaner.

ON THE COVER: *Bertha Honoré Palmer in 1906 in a gown probably made
by Charles Frederick Worth, the father of haute couture. It is a two-piece
evening gown consisting of a bodice and skirt. (Courtesy of Pauline Wood Egan,
Mrs. Palmer's great-granddaughter)*

ACKNOWLEDGEMENTS

SPECIAL THANK YOU to my husband John, and children Amy Lou, Elizabeth and Will for all of their help and understanding as I pursued my "Chicago project" over the course of eight years.

So many friends, too numerous to mention, encouraged me to write a story about Mrs. Potter Palmer. Several provided immeasurable help: Pauline Wood Egan, Laurie Bay, Kathryn Johnson, Robin Lee, Caroline Freivogel, Vaughan Lacaillade, Robert Herbst, Rob Medina, Timothy Long, Bill Tyre, Deborah and William Sexton.

Thanks most especially to my mother, Margot Sexton, another "Mrs. Potter Palmer."

Thank you for making this book possible.

Sally Sexton Kalmbach

Mr. Arthur Wood sitting beneath an original Mary Cassatt print purchased by Mrs. Potter Palmer in 1892.

IN MEMORY OF MR. ARTHUR WOOD

 N SEPTEMBER OF 2002 I started on what I termed my "Chicago project," a walking tour of the Gold Coast highlighting the life of Mrs. Potter Palmer. I called my friend Pauline Wood Egan (Mrs. Palmer's great-granddaughter) to ask what she thought of the idea, if she had any pictures of Bertha Palmer, and if she would share any interesting stories. She told me one about the Palmer House dining room, but then suggested that I visit her father, Mr. Arthur Wood, in his home in Lake Forest to view the Palmer scrapbooks.

There was an abundance of information in the scrapbooks, and it became quite clear that what I thought of as a day of reading would require a number of visits. Mr. Wood seemed delighted that I would return to complete my research, but neither of us anticipated that it would involve weekly visits over the course of a year.

I started looking forward to my day with Mr. Wood, initially for the fascinating Palmer stories, but eventually to talk and laugh with him and enjoy lunch together in his home or at a local restaurant. On numerous occasions he would meet me with an idea: an article, book or story. One morning he said we were going to look through the closets because he thought there might be some pictures of Mrs. Palmer. We started rummaging through the hall closet and uncovered an original Mary Cassatt print!

Always encouraging me to write a story, take pictures of the Palmer artifacts and continue my research, Mr. Wood became my greatest supporter and a wonderful friend. This little book is dedicated to him.

Sally Sexton Kalmbach
May 2009

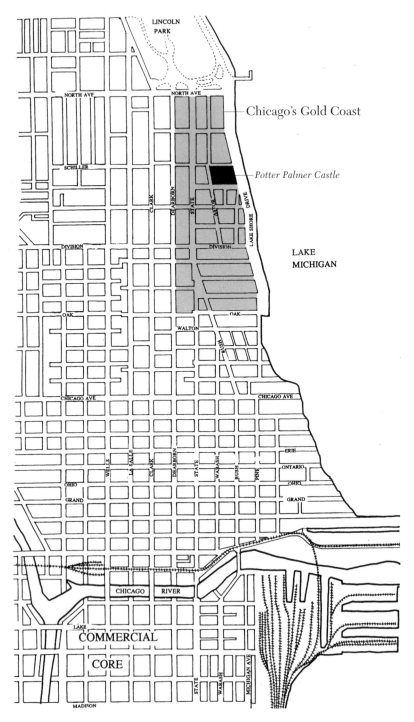

LINCOLN
PARK

NORTH AVE

NORTH AVE

Chicago's Gold Coast

SCHILLER

Potter Palmer Castle

CLARK
DEARBORN
STATE
ASTOR
LAKE SHORE DRIVE

DIVISION

DIVISION

LAKE
MICHIGAN

OAK

OAK

WALTON

RUSH

CHICAGO AVE

CHICAGO AVE

WELLS
LA SALLE
CLARK
DEARBORN
STATE
WABASH
RUSH
PINE

ERIE

ONTARIO

OHIO

OHIO

GRAND

GRAND

CHICAGO RIVER

LAKE

COMMERCIAL

CORE

STATE
WABASH
MICHIGAN AVE

MADISON

Near North Side of Chicago, 1886. (The Charnley House)

CONTENTS

ILLUSTRATIONS

Mrs. Potter Palmer in 1893 in a gown now in the collection of the Chicago History Museum. As was her custom, she is covered in jewels. The three brooches on the neckline – all different – are no longer attached to the gown. The tiara is similar to the crown Anders Zorn painted on Mrs. Palmer in his 1893 portrait of her for the Columbian Exposition. (Courtesy of Pauline Wood Egan)

Chapter 1

SETTING THE STAGE

"Brilliant Wedding in High Life –
Marriage of Potter Palmer and Miss Bertha Honoré"
CHICAGO TRIBUNE
July 29, 1870

ON A WARM DAY in late July of 1870, Bertha Honoré married Potter Palmer at her parents' fashionable limestone home at 157 Michigan Avenue, across the street from today's site of the Art Institute of Chicago.

The tree-lined residential street was filled with carriages depositing the forty relatives and close friends who attended the wedding ceremony.

At 6:00 P.M. a pastor from the First Christian Church performed the ceremony. A wedding supper for seven hundred followed the service, catered by Kinsley's, one of the most celebrated restaurants of the day. Noted for its oysters shipped from the East Coast, Kinsley's was located on Washington Street between Dearborn and State, not far from the Honoré home.

The petite 5'5" dark-eyed woman of 21 was dressed in a gown of white satin and rose-point lace designed by Charles Frederick Worth, a designer who dominated Parisian fashion in the latter half of the nineteenth century. Orange blossoms were arranged in her brown hair. Her small waist was encircled by a corset, an item of clothing in vogue throughout most of her life.

Potter Palmer was a happy man. At the age of 44, he was the most eligible bachelor in Chicago. He had illustrated his business acumen by amassing millions, traveled extensively in Europe, sown his wild oats, and now he was marrying the intelligent and graceful woman who had captured his attention eight years previously.

Her wedding present was the new Palmer House Hotel, valued at $3,500,000, that was being completed at the time of their marriage.[1]

The Honoré home located at 157 Michigan Avenue, across the street from today's site of the Art Institute of Chicago. (Chicago History Museum)

After the ceremony, the newly married couple departed for Europe, but Paris was not part of the itinerary because of the Franco-Prussian war raging in France. This was Bertha's first journey to Europe, but her introduction to Paris and the Impressionists lay in the future.

Both Potter Palmer and the Honoré family settled in Chicago, a wild and dirty prairie town, in the 1850s. Palmer came from a farming family of seven children in Albany County, New York. They farmed at Potter's Hollow, located on the west bank of the Hudson River. Palmer was descended from a Quaker colonial family that arrived in the United States from Britain in 1628 along with John Endicott, first Governor of the Colony of Massachusetts. But Palmer had no interest in continuing

Potter Palmer in 1868 at the age of 42, two years before his marriage to Bertha Honoré. (Courtesy of Pauline Wood Egan)

the farming tradition. With some retail experience in New York and armed with $5,000, a gift from his father, he arrived in Chicago in 1852 to begin his career as a merchant.[2]

Bertha's father, Henry Hamilton Honoré, often referred to as H.H., had moved his family of six children to Chicago from Louisville, Kentucky. His grandfather was Jean Antoine Honoré, who was Parisian and a friend of Lafayette. He later moved to Louisville and operated the first line of steamboats between New Orleans and Louisville.

Bertha's mother, Eliza, was descended from the English family of Edward D'Arcy who had settled in Maryland. When H.H. and Eliza packed up their belongings and moved to Chicago, their families were sorry to see them leave their southern roots for a northern cattle town.

Bertha Honoré was six years old when her family settled in the "Kentucky Colony" on what today is Ashland Avenue, along with fellow Kentuckian, Carter Harrison, who was to serve five terms as Chicago's mayor. H.H. built a large southern colonial house on the southwest corner of Ashland and Jackson for his family, and Bertha was raised in the Southern tradition in this small community. She attended St. Xavier's Academy, Dearborn Seminary, and completed her education at the Convent of the Visitation in Georgetown, Washington, D.C. in 1867, graduating with highest honors. Bertha was an unusually well-educated woman for the time period, when many women in her position were educated at home by private governesses.[3]

She was schooled in the social graces at an early age and became an excellent hostess, helping her parents entertain their guests at their annual New Year's Day reception. She later made this celebration famous during her married life living on Lake Shore Drive. Business and politics were part of her life, as her father discussed his real estate development ideas with her on a regular basis.

She was the eldest of six children and first met Potter Palmer at her family home when she was thirteen years old. Many years later, Palmer, who was twenty-three years older than Bertha, shared with his son Honoré that he was so impressed with the young teen-aged girl that he decided that night to wait until she was older to ask her to marry him.[4]

H.H. Honoré had an interest in local real estate, erecting a large number of office buildings on Dearborn Street, and developing an Ashland Avenue subdivision. The Honoré Building, located at Dearborn and Adams, later housed The Union League Club, a political-social organization that was to become the setting of numerous historical events.

This was a time of aggressive real estate speculation, when lots were traded and heavily mortgaged, and credit was stretched to the maximum. At the time of their meeting, Palmer was running a prosperous dry goods store on Lake Street selling the latest merchandise from Paris. Wealthy women hastened to his store to take advantage of his progressive business practice of offering credit and a liberal exchange policy which became known as the "Palmer System."[5] Merchant representatives from other cities arrived in Chicago to study Palmer's methods, including a large department store in New York called Macy's![6] Palmer helped establish shopping as a delightful pastime between social calls and charitable works.

In 1865, Palmer sold his store to two young retailers, Marshall Field and Levi Leiter. For a time, Palmer provided his name and credit when the store was called Field, Palmer and Leiter, but in 1881 it became Marshall Field & Company.

Initially, Field did not believe Palmer's credit and exchange policies were economically sound, so when he and Leiter took control of the store, they abolished the practice. But Field soon learned the benefits of catering to women and spent much of his career implementing unique attractions, including restaurant facilities and lounging rooms designed to please women shoppers. After the return policy was re-instated, a story circulated about a tablecloth offered for sale by the linen department. Field asked the department head about the Italian import cloth, which cost $800. Field did not think it would ever sell, but he was surprised one night to see it covering the table at a "Mrs. C's," where he was a guest at a dinner party. The next day Field congratulated the department head for selling such an expensive item, to which he replied: "I am sorry to tell you, Mr. Field, that 'Mrs. C' took it yesterday on approval and this morning it came back!"[7]

Palmer had made a fortune trading cotton and wool during the Civil War, and now that he had sold his dry goods store, he began an active real estate career, soon becoming Chicago's largest land owner. He bought land on State Street for $200 a square foot, intending to move the city's center of business from Lake Street, which was dirty, had poor drainage, smelled of the river, and was not suitable as a major business throughfare.[8] He constructed large office buildings, including a six-story emporium on the corner of State and Washington that he rented to Field and Leiter for the sum of $50,000 per year.[9] He also proposed widening State Street from 60 feet to 120 feet to allow frontage for carriages and trolley car tracks.[10]

———

The Palmers had been married just over a year when Chicago, a city constructed of wood, exploded into flames on the night of October 8, 1871. Palmer lost the Palmer House and thirty-five of his other buildings in the Great Chicago Fire. Fortunately, he had such a sterling reputation that he was able to obtain a loan of $1,700,000, which was thought to be the largest personal loan granted at that time, to help re-build his empire.[11]

The newly built Palmer House, completed shortly after the Chicago Fire of 1871, was more luxurious than the first. (Chicago History Museum)

He began re-building with the six-story Palmer House, making it more luxurious than the original, even to the extent of embedding silver dollars in the floor of the barbershop. But if you are thinking that sounds terribly extravagant, according to a Palmer family member, the silver dollars had been cut in half before being installed.[12] Through the prescience of the accomplished architect, John M. Van Osdel, the blueprints of the earlier Palmer House had been saved, buried deep in the basement under layers of clay and sand. Construction began immediately with the crew working night shifts to complete the job in a timely manner.

The most frequently used adjective in 1872 was "fire-proof." The City Council outlawed wooden buildings in the downtown area and passed an additional ordinance that only brick or stone buildings could be erected in the business district.[13] In 1874 Potter Palmer challenged the public to set fire to a room in the newly built Palmer House to test the theory that his building was in fact fire-proof. No one accepted the challenge.[14]

Joseph Medill, owner and editor of the *Chicago Tribune* and credited with helping to found and name the Republican Party, predicted that Chicago would rise again, but no one realized how quickly. Medill won the mayoralty election following the Fire in 1871 by campaigning on the issue of fire prevention. The city of ashes grew into a metropolis filled with hotels, office buildings, and cultural institutions. One thousand two hundred fifty building permits were granted the first year after the Fire with an expenditure of $38,000,000.[15]

Real estate boomed! During the years following the fire, Chicago in the 1870s was busy rebuilding itself architecturally and socially. Young men were encouraged to travel to Chicago to seek their fortunes in industry, and the population grew rapidly. Expansion was felt on every level: the Grand Pacific Hotel, Palmer House, Sherman House and Tremont House opened their new doors for business. The Palmer House stables were proclaimed the best in the northwest, and two new coaches were purchased to convey guests to and from the hotel. North side streetcars crossed the Chicago River for the first time in 1873, while the north side Park Commissioners were purchasing a strip of land from Bishop Foley to build an extension of Lake Shore Drive from Lincoln Park.

The Chicago Literary Club, Fortnightly Club, Chicago Woman's Club and the Commercial Club were founded in the 1870s, and the Chicago Club was moving to its new home opposite the Palmer House. All of these clubs are still active today, with the exception of the Chicago Woman's Club. A number of reform associations and committees were established to clean up the city's graft and corruption, but not a great deal was accomplished. The closing of saloons on Sunday and the selling of liquor to minors became hot issues.

Several newspapers were in print: *Chicago Daily News*, *Saturday Evening Herald*, and *Sunday Sun*. They reported the important news of the era: Edison's phonograph, Bell's first telephone exchange in New Haven in 1877, and Edison's lighting his laboratory and houses in Menlo Park with electricity. In the late 1870s Theodore Thomas started an orchestra to play classical music, and the Academy of Fine Arts was organized, eventually becoming the Art Institute of Chicago. Montgomery Ward began a mail order business in 1872, and when the Chicago Council approved the sale of lakefront property to the Illinois Central Railroad for $800,000, he began a crusade to protect the lakefront, becoming one of Chicago's heroes. But he never anticipated that his court battle would last twenty years and cost him personally a great deal of money. He single-handedly tried to keep the lakefront "open, clear and free" as promised when the city was first incorporated.

A man named J.J. Wallace wrote a letter to the *Tribune* and asked, "Who shall set a value on his service? The present generation, I believe, hardly appreciates what has been given them, but those who come later, as they avail themselves of the breathing spot, will realize it."[16] It would be interesting to hear Montgomery Ward's thoughts about the lakefront today.

It was not until 1880 that Cook County Hospital opened the first nursing school and the cornerstone of Rush Medical College was laid. Lake Michigan's water was still contaminated. Numerous deaths each year were attributed to outbreaks of cholera, diphtheria and typhus. Healthcare had a long journey ahead as Chicago entered a new decade with more than 500,000 residents.

The Financial Panic of 1873 had led to the suspension of five banks and caused people to be placed on relief, but Chicago was able to weather the financial storm due to the flood of hogs, cattle, wheat, and corn pouring into the city.

Potter Palmer, Cyrus McCormick and other influential Chicagoans helped raise the money to build the Inter-State Exposition Building of 1873 to serve as a center for music, art, commerce, and industry. It was made of wood, brick, and glass, designed by W.W. Boyington and similar in style to the 1851 Crystal Palace in London. Numerous exhibits were held in this modern edifice during a time when Chicago was growing into an important commercial center.

In 1879, the Exposition introduced summer night concerts led by the Theodore Thomas orchestra, hosted the exciting Republican Convention of 1880 where Garfield was nominated, and even housed Marshall Field and Levi Leiter's merchandise when a fire broke out in their State Street department store. A large German beer garden and a winter ice skating rink were popular Exposition venues.

Monet, Pissarro and Degas were represented at the 1890 Art Exposition show orchestrated by Sara Hallowell, who later became the Palmers' art agent. Harriet Monroe, founder of *Poetry Magazine*, wrote in *Art Amateur* that she was impressed with most of the Impressionist canvases, but thought some were blotchy with clashing colors.

The Exposition building was razed in 1892 to make way for the new building that hosted the World Congresses during the Columbian Exposition of 1893. At the close of the Fair, this new building became the Art Institute of Chicago.

———————

The Inter-State Exposition Building of 1873 served as a center for music, art, commerce and industry. This building was razed in 1892 to make way for the building that hosted the World Congress during the Columbian Exposition of 1893. At the close of the Fair, the building became the Art Institute of Chicago. (Chicago History Museum)

In 1874 several changes were brought to Mrs. Potter Palmer, nicknamed "Cissie" by her husband. She moved into the newly built Palmer House, gave birth to their first son, Honoré, and established herself as Chicago's first lady, leading a society that had not existed prior to the Chicago Fire. She co-coordinated her younger sister Ida's wedding to Frederick Grant, the son of Ulysses S. Grant. The association with the Grant family led the Palmers to frequent trips to the White House on social and state occasions. When President Grant visited Chicago, he would stay at the celebrated Palmer House and the Palmers would entertain him.

On one occasion, when President Grant was visiting Chicago with his wife, a reception was scheduled at the Chicago Club. Since Mrs. Grant was accompanying the President, the wives of club members, normally not welcome at the club, were invited. A few days before the event, a Chicago Club member phoned the President of the club asking if he could bring his mistress! The Club President responded quickly: "Why certainly, as long as she is the wife of a member!"[17]

President Grant reportedly offered the post of Secretary of Interior to Palmer, but Palmer wasn't interested in a political career or in giving public speeches.[18] He was satisfied with running his real estate empire with his wife, his only true business partner throughout his life.

During her early years of marriage, Mrs. Palmer led a simpler, more domestic life with her two sons, Honoré and Potter, Jr. Entertainment consisted of sleigh rides, picnics, dances, dinner parties in private homes and horse racing at Washington Park. All invitations were hand-written and hand-delivered, which often occupied the better part of a day.

The society columns of the local newspapers kept track of the Palmers' social activities:

Society Gossip
Mr. and Mrs. Potter Palmer are acquainted with
two or three thousand people in Chicago. Only 500 invitations have
been sent for their reception in December of 1877.
How many spiteful comments among the uninvited?
CHICAGO TRIBUNE
December 7, 1877

Mrs. Palmer's evenings were spent in their private quarters in the Palmer House, discussing every aspect of her husband's business. In later years, Mrs. Palmer said everything she knew about business she learned in those early evening discussions.[19]

When, after the Fire, the newly built Palmer House was experiencing difficulties attracting people to the dining room, Potter Palmer thought of lowering the prices. Mrs. Palmer said, "No! Raise the prices and people will flock to the restaurant." He did, and it became one of the most popular places to eat and be seen.[20]

Potter Palmer must have thought of this and numerous other stories when he made out his will in which he left his entire estate to his wife. But his lawyer tried to convince him of an alternative plan, saying, "Your wife is a young woman, she might very well marry again." Whereupon Potter Palmer responded, "If she does, he'll need the money."[21] When his old friend Marshall Field heard that Palmer had left his entire estate to his wife, Field's response was typical of his frugal personality, "A million dollars is enough for any woman!" When Marshall Field died in 1906, leaving an estate worth approximately $120,000,000, he was true to his philosophy. He left his wife, the former Delia Caton, the love of his life, $2,000,000 along with the Field mansion and its contents, with the bulk of his estate going to his grandsons.[22]

Mrs. Palmer became an excellent business woman, and by her death in 1918, she had more than doubled her husband's estate.

This photo was taken in 1900 for the Paris Exposition. The gown was designed by Worth, made of silk net, jet and sequins. (Courtesy of Pauline Wood Egan)

Chapter 2

POTTER PALMER
WALKS NORTH

*Potter Palmer said, "I am going over there, north,
to work out a new residence district."*
"It will fall into the lake," they warned.
Chicago, A Portrait
by Henry Justin Smith, page 30

WHAT ARE TODAY eight to ten lanes of noisy traffic was once a quiet dirt path along the lake. In the late 1870s when Potter Palmer started buying land along the lake just south of Lincoln Park, Chicago residents laughed. This swamp land, or Frog Pond as it was called, was filled with sand, willows, and mud.[1]

Although Palmer had proven his real estate expertise in developing State Street, this new project was sometimes referred to as "Frog's Folly." He filled the marshland with sand taken from Lake Michigan, rightfully assuming it would be cleaner than the refuse normally used during a time when malaria and diphtheria were prevalent.

In the book, *Giants Gone, the Men who Made Chicago*, Ernest Poole tells the story of two young boys who regularly went duck shooting before dawn in this marshland. One day, they saw a tanker anchored off-shore pumping sand from Lake Michigan to fill in the marshland and the boys asked who had hired the dredger. The workers answered: "We have a contract with Potter Palmer to fill in the whole of this big swamp. No more duck shooting for you kids!"[2]

PILE DRIVING AND THE BEGINNING OF CONSTRUCTION OF WHAT WAS TO BE KNOWN AS "LAKE SHORE DRIVE" . . . .

● CONSTRUCTING LAKE SHORE DRIVE FROM THE "FROG POND" — 1882

This 1882 picture of the "Frog Pond" gives a sense of how barren and undesirable this wind-swept area looked before Potter Palmer began developing it. (Chicago History Museum)

While Jean DuSable, the city's first settler, built his house on the north side of the Chicago River in 1779, during the nineteenth century most Chicagoans did not live north of the river. They wanted to be on the same side of the river as their business offices and churches.[3]

Traffic was heavy on the well-traveled Rush Street Bridge across the Chicago River. Bridge tenders were unreliable and there were long delays waiting for the Bridge to be raised.[4] Prior to the building of the Michigan Avenue Bridge in 1920, Rush Street Bridge carried more traffic than London Bridge.

Following the Chicago Fire, Prairie Avenue, one of the longest streets close to both Lake Michigan and the downtown business district, became the most fashionable residential district of Chicago. Located south of the river and east of Michigan Avenue, it attracted the families of the leading merchants of the day. George Pullman, P.D. Armour, Marshall Field and William Kimball all built large mansions in this first "silk stocking" area of 16th to 22nd Streets which, according to Mrs. Arthur Meeker, comprised "the Sunny Street that held the Sifted Few."[5]

Downtown Chicago was a nightmare, as seen in this traffic jam on Dearborn Street. (Chicago History Museum)

Prairie Avenue represented the height of society neighborhoods until the 1880s when Potter Palmer's predictions were proven correct. By this time, the residents had tired of the soot and dirty air from the Illinois Central railroad and the stockyards in the commercial district.

Though real estate agent Henry C. Jefferson had written a pamphlet as early as 1873 emphasizing the desirability of moving to the North Side, it was the actual construction of the boulevard that was to become Lake Shore Drive that spurred the migration toward Palmer's progressive real estate vision. By 1875, a road 200 feet wide and three quarters of a mile long had been built and named Lake Drive.[6]

After buying large amounts of land from the Water Tower continuing north and west, Palmer then sold lots to friends and business acquaintances and offered building incentives to those who completed their homes in a timely manner. He built speculative homes, rental properties, and apartment buildings in the area that became known as the Gold Coast. He worked with the Lincoln Park Board of Commissions to build Lake Drive and later he helped name it Lake Shore Drive as a northern extension of Pine Street, which today is North Michigan

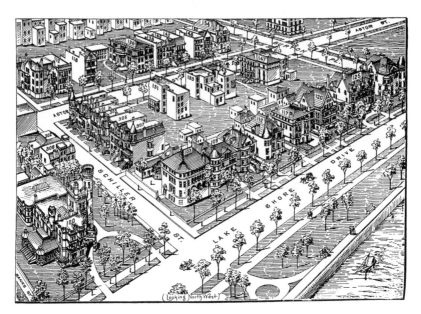

Aerial view looking northwest from the east side of Lake Shore Drive at Banks Street in 1893, after Potter Palmer developed the area. The Palmer "castle" is building 100, between Banks and Schiller Streets. (Rand McNally's Bird's-Eye Views and Guide to Chicago, 1897)

Avenue. It wasn't until 1946 that the entire drive from downtown continuing north was called Lake Shore Drive.

Palmer preferred the cool air, summer breezes, and unobstructed view of Lake Michigan in the area called the Frog Pond. By the turn of the century, the Frog Pond had become the city's most valuable real estate.

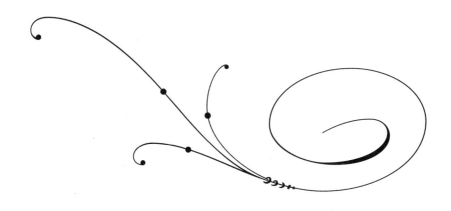

Mrs. Palmer's gown, made by Worth, is in the collection of the Chicago History Museum. It is silk velvet, woven with a satin corn pattern – perfect for "The Princess of the Prairie." She is wearing her famous pink pearl. (Courtesy of Pauline Wood Egan)

POTTER PALMER BUILDS
HIS DREAM HOUSE

*"Frequenters of the North Shore Drive are now able to form a
pretty good opinion of what Potter Palmer's palace will look like
when completed as it is ready for the roof and many of the turreted
towers that will give it the appearance of a castle..."*
CHICAGO DAILY TRIBUNE
September 9, 1883

OR HIS OWN family, Potter Palmer built a great baronial castle of no particular architectural style, although it was referred to as "the monstrosity" or the castle plucked from a goldfish bowl. Located on Lake Shore Drive, it occupied the entire block from Banks to Schiller Streets, land once owned by John Jacob Astor that Palmer had purchased for a modest sum.[1]

Built in 1882 and designed by Henry Ives Cobb (who also designed the Newberry Library, many of the buildings at the University of Chicago, and numerous others) and Charles Sumner Frost, it was made of Wisconsin granite and Ohio sandstone, not to Mrs. Palmer's liking, but age and a lacework of English ivy mellowed its appearance. The eighty foot tower was its most dramatic feature. It was where the quiet Potter Palmer used to escape from Mrs. Palmer's many social events, and it contained the first private elevators in Chicago.

The house was constructed with no exterior doorknobs or locks so a servant had to admit guests. A calling card had to pass through the hands of 27 maids, butlers and social secretaries, and even Mrs. Palmer's closest friends were required to write in advance for an appointment.[2]

Initially, the castle was to cost in the neighborhood of $90,000, but when the bills reached close to $750,000 Potter Palmer asked his bookkeeper to stop entering the charges.[3] When the castle was completed in 1885, it had taken three years and cost $1,000,000. It set the tone of ostentation in the neighborhood. Francis Webber Sever, a Harvard graduate visiting the Columbian Exposition of 1893, wrote to his aunt: "I saw Potter Palmer's house, a monstrous house in the worst taste – brown and green stone, turreted."[4]

But Mr. Pullman said to Dr. Nin of Uruguay, "Every man's house is his castle in Chicago." Arthur Meeker, author of *To Chicago, with Love* said, "During the 1880s and '90s taste in America, we must admit, was as bad as it ever was."

The home's interior was a mixture of styles: French drawing room, Victorian library, Spanish music room, English dining room. The three story octagonal entry hall contained a floor of mosaic marble that Boston architect Henry Hobson Richardson thought to be "the handsomest in the country." [5] The lions that adorned the newel posts on the stairway are a few of the salvaged items from the house.

The dining room was used regularly to entertain as many as fifty at a seated dinner and contained Potter Palmer's favorite portrait of Mrs. Palmer, painted in her youth by George P.A. Healy. The ninety foot long combination ballroom and picture gallery that was added in 1893 was designed by Henry Hardenbergh, who also designed the Dakota Apartments and Plaza Hotel in New York. It became the most famous room in the house, where Mrs. Potter Palmer's paintings hung in tiers according to schools against a red velvet background. She was considered a pioneer among Impressionist art collectors, and was among the first to bring Impressionist art to the United States, but definitely the first to the mid-west.

Mrs. Palmer said, "Keep up with the procession is my motto, and head it if you can. I do head it, and I feel that I'm where I belong."
The Proud Possessors
by Aline B. Saarinen, page 4

The Palmer Castle quickly became the most famous house in the city, where Mrs. Palmer entertained constantly, always dressed in the latest Worth gown from Paris. Her priceless jewelry was rivaled only by the collections of members of royalty. Palmer regularly purchased Mrs. Palmer's favorites – pearls and diamonds – but the most extravagant piece was a seven-strand dog collar with over two thousand pearls

When the Potter Palmer "castle" was completed in 1885 it had taken three years and cost one million dollars. (Chicago History Museum)

Baluster salvaged from the Castle's main staircase. (Courtesy of Mr. William Tyre)

One of two lions that adorned the newel posts on the Palmer stairway. (Courtesy of Mr. Arthur Wood)

The three story octagonal entry hall of the Palmer castle contained a floor of mosaic marble admired by architect Henry Hobson Richardson. (Chicago History Museum)

and seven diamonds. Watching from a distance, Potter would remark, "There she stands with two hundred thousand dollars on her."[6]

"Art is like fashion," Mrs. Palmer explained to a woman's group. "The more you put on, sometimes, the worse you look, and the more you take off, the better you look."[7] She rarely followed her own advice!

Her friend, Mrs. Carter Harrison, Jr., wrote that she never knew a woman to handle a heavy load of jewelry as gracefully as Mrs. Palmer.[8]

Her New Year's Day reception became the most prestigious invitation in Chicago. To be asked to this event meant that one was accepted in society the following year and would certainly receive an invitation to Mrs. Palmer's famous Charity Ball. Proceeds from the Ball went to several different institutions, and it was usually held at the Auditorium Theater, designed by Adler and Sullivan in 1889. The *Kansas City Star* reported that Mrs. Palmer had always looked upon society as a business.[9]

She made the castle available on numerous occasions, including meetings and lectures to educate working girls. When the meetings were completed, she often gave the women a tour of her art gallery.

In 1892, Mrs. Potter Palmer opened her home for the Columbian Bazaar to raise money for the Children's Building at the Columbian Exposition. The bazaar was a miniature fair. Although it was reported that a few silver spoons went missing, it raised the needed $35,000 in three days with 8,000 people attending. The Children's Building offered babysitting services for working women (a precursor to daycare), contained an elaborate gymnasium, and exhibited educational materials for kindergartens, which were becoming very popular in the United States.

During the Columbian Exposition, Mrs. Palmer hosted a dinner for Princess Eulalia, the official representative of the Queen Regent of Spain and the highest ranking royal person attending the Fair. The cream of Chicago society and the exposition officials were invited to the dinner. The young princess had previously breakfasted with the Carter Harrisons and dined with the Harlow Higinbothams (President of the Fair), but she was not interested in attending a reception held by an "innkeeper's wife." Convinced by the Spanish ambassador that she must attend, Princess Eulalia arrived at the Lake Shore Drive castle in a bad temper. She barely acknowledged the guests, exchanged a few words with Mrs. Palmer and left before the supper was served.

The newspapers across the country had a field day with the event and some exaggerated stories emerged. Mrs. Palmer wrote a note to Mr. Gresham of the State Department complaining about the snub. Mr. Gresham replied, "The Infanta treated you and other Chicago people with gross impoliteness, and I feel indignant about it."[10]

Mrs. Palmer was a great advocate for women's rights in the area of education, equal pay for equal work and improving working conditions, but she was not a suffragist. She felt that intelligent women could work with men to achieve their goals rather than campaigning for the right to vote. Maybe had she lived into the 1920s, Bertha would have altered her opinion on this issue, but diplomacy was her preferred method of balancing the social and working worlds.

Official Souvenir Programme from the Columbian Exposition Dedication Ceremony.
(Chicago History Museum)

The Fortnightly Club was founded in 1873 and is considered the first woman's club in Chicago. Today, The Fortnightly occupies the former Byron Lathrop house, designed by Charles F. McKim. (Courtesy of Professor Lynn Westley)

While the population of Chicago was growing dramatically – doubling from 1880 to 1890 – the number of women's clubs also grew and the clubs became influential in society and with working women. The Fortnightly Club was founded in 1873 by Kate Doggett and is considered the first women's club in Chicago. In April of 1873 she asked a number of women to meet at her home at 3:00 P.M. precisely for an hour's talk about a project that greatly interested her.[11] Doggett was passionate about intellectual growth and was interested in bringing together a group of women to discuss and write papers about the arts and women's history. The Club exists today in the historic Byron Lathrop house, designed by Charles F. McKim.

McKim (of the firm McKim, Mead & White) was a friend of the Lathrop family who traveled to Chicago to design the Architectural Building for the Columbian Exposition and, at the same time, designed the Lathrop house. It is considered one of the best examples of the Georgian Revival style.

Bertha Palmer joined The Fortnightly in 1880, and during the planning of the Columbian Exposition she read a preview paper, paving the way for the numerous speeches she would give as Chairman of the

Board of the Lady Managers. Many Fortnightly members were involved in planning for the World's Congress, a series of over two hundred lectures/meetings held in the Art Palace located on Michigan Avenue. The first was entitled "Dress Reform!"

Mrs. Palmer and Jane Addams of Hull House joined the Chicago Woman's Club that was established to study social problems, largely for the protection of women and children.[12] Mrs. Palmer helped organize the Chicago Woman's Business Club in 1888 to assist the growing number of women entering the work force as operators of the telephone and typewriter. In the 1890s Mrs. Palmer served as vice-president of the Civic Federation, established to bring capital and labor together. During this time she helped the milliners form their first union.[13]

Charles Hutchinson, banker and art collector, who had become president of the Art Institute in 1882 (and served until his death in 1924), proposed a new building for the Art Institute to be opened at the close of the Columbian Exposition. The Art Palace, designed by Shepley, Rutan & Coolidge, was converted into an art museum for Chicago. The city's cultural life benefited from hosting the Exposition because part of the funding for the museum came from Exposition proceeds.

> "It is hopeless for the occasional visitor to try to keep up with
> Chicago – she outgrows his prophecies faster than he can
> make them. She is always a novelty; for she is never the Chicago
> you saw when you passed through last time."
>
> MARK TWAIN,
> Life on the Mississippi, 1883

During the 1880s while Mrs. Palmer was busy entertaining in her castle and pursuing her philanthropic pursuits, Chicago was experiencing the springtime of inventions. The phonograph was patented, electricity was in the making, and a city telephone book was published with 250 names. But the ritual of the gas lighting hour at dusk by a street lighter continued. The cable car arrived in Chicago, and commercial architecture was booming with the invention of the elevator and John Root's "floating foundation" which was used in the construction of the Montauk Block, Rookery and Monadnock buildings.

Author Thomas Tallmadge wrote, "What Chartres was to the Gothic Cathedral, the Montauk Block was to the high commercial building" because of the revolutionary new building method; it was the first fire-proof tall building ever constructed.[14]

Root understood the driving force of business enterprise and, according to real estate lawyer Owen Aldis, who obtained many commissions for the architect, Root was a genius.

This time period was often referred to as the "elegant eighties," but in fact the city was plagued by strikers fighting for the eight hour workday.[15] The McCormick Reaper Works strike, streetcar and railroad strikes culminated in the Haymarket Riot, when an unidentified person threw a bomb at a Union Labor rally in 1886, killing seven policemen.

In the midst of this confusion, a new city was emerging with fifteen thousand miles of railroad that brought workers to Chicago while Fort Sheridan was being built along the lakefront to protect Chicagoans from future attacks from anarchists.[16]

Taken about 1900, this gown, also by Worth, has a stunning asymmetrical embroidered flora and fauna motif. Her jeweled collar is believed to be by Tiffany. (Courtesy of Pauline Wood Egan)

NEIGHBORHOOD
DEVELOPMENT

*"When Potter Palmer sold me the land in 1885 where my house now
stands there were only two other houses there – the Palmer home
and the little red house then belonging to James Charnley, which
stood at Division Street and the Drive. Doctors said the location
was unhealthful, that the lake breezes were dangerous. I improved
in health from the time I moved into the house from the south side."*

FRANKLIN MACVEAGH,
Secretary of Treasury under Taft
Chicago Tribune July 1915

THE AREA KNOWN as the Gold Coast centered around the
Potter Palmers' "English Gothic" castle on Lake Shore Drive. The
social world began migrating north to settle in what was then a wild and
windswept area. When Palmer started buying lake frontage property
in the early 1880s he paid $160 a front foot. By the time many of his
friends and business acquaintances were moving into the area in 1892
the price had skyrocketed to $800 a front foot.[1]

In 1885, when the castle was completed, there were only two other
residences on Lake Shore Drive. The first was the James Charnley family's home, designed by Burnham & Root in 1882 and located at Lake
Shore Drive and Division Street. The other residence to grace Lake
Shore Drive was the William Borden mansion, designed in 1884 by the
leading architect of the day, Richard Morris Hunt, but not completed
until 1886. The limestone French Renaissance chateau closely resem-
bled the Vanderbilt mansion on Fifth Avenue that Hunt had recently
designed. Hunt also designed the Administration Building, thought

The James Charnley house, designed by Burnham & Root in 1882, was the first house on Lake Shore Drive. (Chicago History Museum)

The William Borden mansion was designed by Richard Morris Hunt and completed in 1886. It was razed in the early 1960s. (Chicago History Museum)

The former home of Edith Rockefeller McCormick was designed by Solon S. Beman and was demolished in 1953. (Chicago History Museum)

by many to be one of the most beautiful buildings at the Columbian Exposition of 1893.

William Borden, along with Potter Palmer, had also purchased land along Lake Shore Drive which he subdivided and sold. The Borden mansion was demolished in the 1960s.

1000 Lake Shore Drive, now a modern apartment building, was the site of the home of Edith Rockefeller McCormick. Mr. and Mrs. Potter Palmer were already living in their castle when the forty-one room mansion was designed for Nathanial Jones by the young Solon S. Beman in 1888. Beman arrived in Chicago to execute several commissions for George Pullman of the Pullman Railway Company. Beman designed the town of Pullman, the downtown Pullman office buildings, private residences, and the Mines Building of the Columbian Exposition. After completing the town of Pullman, Beman suggested to Pullman that the town be named after him, Beman. Pullman thought about this and quickly responded, "Why don't we use the first part of my name and the last part of your name and call it Pullman!"[2]

The elaborate gates to the McCormick property were a gift from the German Kaiser to his country's exhibition at the Columbian Exposition.

At the close of the Fair, General Torrence, then owner of the house, purchased the gates and had a matching fence built around the entire property. When the house was being demolished in 1953, the gates were put up for sale. They were valued at $150,000, but the highest bid was $4,700. They were sold to the Buchanan Iron and Metal Company in Michigan. The firm did offer the fence to anyone who would pay for its removal and future erection, but no one was interested. One of Chicago's finest examples of Victorian hand wrought iron became scrap at a construction site.

In 1895, the Torrence mansion was bought by John D. Rockefeller as a wedding gift for his daughter, Edith, when she married Harold McCormick, son of Cyrus McCormick. John D. Rockefeller provided the bulk of the money to help William Rainy Harper begin the University of Chicago in 1892. The following year in 1893, the year of the Columbian Exposition, the University received a letter addressed: University of Chicago, near the Ferris Wheel!

Edith lived a rather lavish lifestyle. Her father, John D. did not approve, but she was a great philanthropist, single-handedly supporting the Opera by never failing to guarantee the annual deficit. She was an intellectual, but a somewhat peculiar woman. She believed she had lived in a former life, announcing at one dinner party that she had formerly been King Tut's wife! Mrs. Carter Harrison, Jr. wrote about the incident in her book entitled, *Strange to Say.* The guests were a bit shocked, but then "Edith was so brilliant!"

A woman of untold millions, Edith was unable to pay her extraordinary debts at the end of her life. She moved into the Drake Hotel, referred to as the base of the Gold Coast, in 1930, two years before she died.

The MacVeagh House, which set the tone for architectural importance in the neighborhood, was located on the northwest corner of Schiller Street and Lake Shore Drive, across the street from the Palmer's castle. They were close friends of the Palmers, purchased their lot from Potter, and built their house in 1886, one year after the castle was completed. It was designed by the well-known Boston architect Henry Hobson Richardson, who became one of the most important architects of his generation.

Richardson was inspired by the Romanesque style, but developed his own interpretation which was referred to as "Richardsonian Romanesque." Richardson was working on the downtown Marshall

The elaborate gates pictured in the Manufacturers and Liberal Arts Building were a gift from the German Kaiser to his country's exhibition at the Columbian Exhibition of 1893. (Chicago History Museum)

At the close of the Fair, the gates were purchased and transferred to what is now 1000 Lake Shore Drive. A matching fence was built around the entire property. (Chicago History Museum)

The Franklin MacVeagh house was designed by Henry Hobson Richardson in 1886.
This view is looking north from Schiller Street and Lake Shore Drive.
(Chicago History Museum)

Field Warehouse building, the Glessner House, and the MacVeagh house at the same time when he died in 1886 at the young age of 47.

The half-mile stretch of Astor Street just west of the lake has been part of Chicago since the city was incorporated in 1837. Named after John Jacob Astor who founded the American Fur Company in the early 1800s, it was sparsely if at all populated before the Chicago Fire. Originally this area was a Catholic cemetery, bounded by Schiller Street and North Avenue between Lake Shore Drive and State Street. In 1866, largely due to the influence of Dr. John Rauch, a public-spirited physician, the majority of the bodies were moved from the Catholic and City Cemeteries (City Cemetery located in Lincoln Park) to Graceland and Rosehill Cemeteries. The old graves were shallow. Most of the victims had died of small pox, cholera, or other infectious diseases and the area was considered a health risk. Threat of the plague and the desire for a recreational area influenced the City Council to vote to move the bodies. Dr. Rauch was increasingly concerned, since the City's Health Department had been abolished in 1860 and its responsibilities transferred to the Police Department![3] But many of the 20,000 bodies were

*Looking south on Astor Street. John Root houses are at the end of the block.
(Chicago History Museum)*

never removed. When Louise de Koven Bowen was building her home at 1430 North Astor, bones kept cropping up and the servants became nervous. They thought the house was haunted.[4]

Mrs. Bowen recalled the earlier opening of Lincoln Park from a family outing. "It had been a graveyard, and as we drove through it we saw countless open graves with a piece here and there of a decayed coffin, and every now and then on a pile of dirt a bone, evidently dropped by those removing the bodies. As we stand now on Astor Street with its great shade trees on either side, and its beautiful houses, and look north toward Lincoln Park, we find it difficult to realize that this street was once only a sandy beach which had been used as a cemetery."[5]

The large Couch mausoleum still stands in Lincoln Park as well as the grave of David Kenniston, a soldier from Fort Dearborn who died at the age of 115![6]

When the Chicago Historical Society (now the Chicago History Museum) was being built in 1932, more bodies were uncovered.

The first house on Astor Street was built for Archbishop Patrick A. Feehan. In 1880 the Catholic Church hired Alfred Pashley to design

The Patterson-McCormick mansion on the northwest corner of Astor and Burton was commissioned in 1892 by Joseph Medill, owner and editor of the Chicago Tribune, *as a gift to his daughter, Elinor, and her husband, Robert Patterson.*
(Chicago History Museum)

what became known as The Cardinal's Residence, and afterward sold some of their land to Potter Palmer. Constructed of brick and sandstone in the Queen Anne style, with turrets, gables, dormers, and nineteen chimneys, it anchors the block today.

The wooden alley south of the Cardinal's Residence is one of two surviving in Chicago. The six inch cedar blocks were treated with creosote, embedded in the road and filled in with hot tar and gravel. This method of paving was developed by Boston builder Samuel Nicholson in 1848. It was less expensive than cobblestone and much quieter at a time when horses were the primary means of transportation. By the 1890s, close to 65 percent of the city was still paved in this manner.[7]

The Patterson-McCormick mansion on the northwest corner of Astor and Burton was commissioned in 1892 by Joseph Medill, owner/ editor of the *Chicago Tribune*, as a gift to his daughter, Elinor, and her husband Robert Patterson. The story circulated for years that it was a

Astor Street in 1891 with its unpaved street, wooden sidewalk and very few trees. (Chicago History Museum)

wedding gift, but since the Pattersons had been married fourteen years before, it is highly unlikely!

The Pattersons were quite comfortable in the ninety-one room Italian Palazzo designed by the well-known architect Stanford White. During the Patterson years in the mansion their daughter, Eleanor, and son, Joseph, roamed the Gold Coast neighborhood, attended the Columbian Exposition of 1893, and enjoyed the new dessert served on the Fair grounds called an "ice cream sundae."

As a young girl, Eleanor met Mrs. Palmer, who became her model of a strong woman. Coincidentally, Eleanor's brother, Joseph, had called her "Cissy," a nickname also attached to Bertha Palmer.

In the winter of 1901, Eleanor made her debut in the Patterson mansion, dressed in a Worth gown from Paris and jewels from Cartier; as resplendent as Mrs. Palmer at her New Year's soirees!

When the Pattersons moved to Washington, D.C. in 1905 to pursue a more active social and political life, they hired Stanford White

Five speculative Romanesque revival homes were built by Potter Palmer in 1889. The large, sprawling corner house on Astor and Banks was owned by the well-known architect, Ernest Graham, during the 1920s. (Courtesy of Professor Lynn Westley)

When the colonial style Bowen house was being built in 1891, bones kept cropping up because the area was once a Catholic cemetery. (Chicago History Museum)

to design their marble palace on DuPont Circle. At the time, White was still an active architect. However, in 1906 he was murdered in New York by the jealous husband of "The Girl on the Golden Trapeze!"

The house in Chicago was eventually purchased by Cyrus McCormick, Jr. in 1914. In 1928, architect David Adler doubled the size of the house, building a wing at the rear of the property for the McCormick art collection, additional service area, and quarters for his son.

In 1950, the Bateman School bought the property and moved from the Edith Rockefeller McCormick mansion on Lake Shore Drive to its new home on Astor Street. The students who attended Bateman during this time must have had a few tales to tell, having attended school in two such historic homes.

Avoiding demolition in the early 1970s, the McCormick home was turned into condominiums in 1978, and it remains the only Stanford White designed house in the city of Chicago.

William Le Baron Jenney, the "father of the skyscraper" and designer of the Home Insurance Building, the world's first iron-skeleton skyscraper, designed 1427 North Astor in 1889.[8]

1429 North Astor, a derivation of the Romanesque style, was designed in 1890 by Pond & Pond, two brothers from Michigan, who combined elements of many designs to create a charming home. In 1885, a group of townhouses on Schiller Street, some of the earliest dwellings in the newly developed Gold Coast, were designed by H.M. Hanson. Today, the corner house (northwest corner of Schiller and Astor) has changed considerably from what, at the time, was described by Mrs. Carter Harrison, Jr. during the 1890s as a modest, narrow home.

After Mayor Carter Harrison was assassinated at the close of the Columbian Exposition of 1893, his son, Carter, and wife, Edith, moved to Schiller Street. They spent twelve years in this house and "Astor Street Days" are recalled in Mrs. Harrison's book entitled *Strange to Say*. Their view of Lake Michigan and the Palmer castle was unobstructed. During the warm months the rug came out at 4:00 P.M. and the front steps were used to get a breath of fresh air. The neighbors followed suit and it became a regular social event.

This was the era of card parties, sleigh rides, hand-written invitations, and Mrs. Palmer's Monday and Thursday dinner parties. Mrs. Harrison said she regretted the passing of the old horse-drawn cable car. It would travel down Rush Street to the shopping area, and the slow pace made a wonderful time to gossip with friends.

Life seemed less complicated in the 1890s, with time to spare. The telephone and electric light had been invented, but no one could anticipate what lay ahead. In 1949, Mrs. Harrison said, "The mad rush of today was not yet upon us." What would she say in 2009?

During the years that the Harrisons lived on Schiller Street, Carter, Jr. ran for Mayor of Chicago. One day at a large luncheon held at a local hotel, a friend of Mrs. Harrison's announced that there were quite a few women who were not going to vote for her husband in the mayoral election. They thought their decision was best for Chicago. Mrs. Harrison said she understood perfectly, but "When the vote is cast the campaign will not even notice the absence of the Gold Coast!"[9]

In 1889 five speculative Romanesque revival homes were built on Astor Street by Potter Palmer. They were designed by his architect, Charles Palmer (no relation to the family). In Arthur Meeker's book, *To Chicago, with Love,* he dismissively referred to these "Palmer Houses" (over 100 built by Palmer) as "dark, depressing, and inconvenient." Later he said the entire area should have been named "Palmerville." Instead of the Gold Coast?

The large sprawling corner house at Astor and Banks was owned by Ernest Graham in the 1920s. He had become Daniel Burnham's partner after the Columbian Exposition. Following Burnham's death, Graham re-organized the firm to become Graham, Anderson, Probst and White. When Graham died he left a bequest to create the Graham Foundation, headquartered on North State Parkway in the Madlener house today. Graham designed the Shedd Aquarium, Field Museum, Merchandise Mart, Wrigley Building and numerous other buildings. It has been said that Mr. Graham participated in the construction of more buildings than any architect since Sir Christopher Wren. Because of the increase in the population – by 1890 there were a million residents in Chicago – construction boomed in both commercial and residential dwellings.

In 1891, the Bowen house was designed by Frank Whitehouse in the Colonial style. At the time, it was thought to be very plain because French architecture was becoming the rage. In Mrs. Bowen's autobiography entitled *Growing Up with a City* she wrote that her friends often referred to her house as "the jail." Mrs. Bowen grew up as Louise de Koven, next door neighbor to Kate Doggett, founder of The Fortnightly Club. She married Joseph Bowen, a successful businessman, and devoted her entire life to championing women's and children's rights. She, along with Mrs. Palmer, helped establish the first juvenile court in

When Louise deKoven Bowen's daughter, Helen, married William McCormick Blair in 1912, they hired Arthur Huen to design this Georgian style home next door to her parents. (Chicago History Museum)

The James Charnley family purchased a lot on Astor Street in 1891 and hired Louis Sullivan to design their new home. (Courtesy of Professor Lynn Westley)

John Root designed a group of townhouses in the 1300 block of Astor Street. When they were completed in 1887, Root moved his family into 1310. (Courtesy of Professor Lynn Westley)

the United States. Mrs. Bowen gave numerous speeches for organizations and was once introduced as the speaker who would talk on the prevention of children instead of the protection![10]

She worked tirelessly for Hull House for over forty years, serving as secretary and president of the Woman's Club and contributing financially by building a 72-acre camp for the children of the Hull House neighborhood. Her house was demolished in 1971, four years before Astor Street became an historic district.

When Louise de Koven Bowen's daughter, Helen, married William McCormick Blair in 1912 they hired Arthur Huen (who worked for Frank Whitehouse) to design their Georgian style home at 1416 North Astor. The two families shared a large garden that was used for numerous activities, including ice skating in the winter. The house's moment of political glory came in 1952 when Adlai Stevenson was staying with the Blairs and received the Democratic nomination for President. He walked across the garden and accepted the nomination from Mrs. Bowen's portico. She might not have been pleased because she was a lifelong Republican! She died the following year in 1953 at the age of 94.

In 1890 James Charnley purchased property on Astor and Schiller streets for $27,500. He sub-divided it into four lots, sold three for $27,450 and hired his good friend, Louis Sullivan, to build his family home on the corner lot.[11] The result was one of the most talked about homes in the neighborhood, vastly different from the Romanesque and Queen Anne style homes of the Gold Coast. The new horizontal house was considered revolutionary. Consisting of two large cubes at each end with a third connecting cube, it illustrated mass in its simplest form.

At the time the house was designed, Frank Lloyd Wright was working as Sullivan's chief draftsman, so there were definitely design ideas attributed to Wright. As downtown Chicago was growing vertically, with the skyscrapers of the 1880s, Sullivan's horizontal house in the Gold Coast was an intriguing addition.

A few blocks south, the Elizabethan-feeling red sandstone and brick townhouses at 1308–1310 North Astor were designed by Burnham & Root, attributed to John Root, who lived at 1310, when they were completed in 1887.

John Root was one of the great architects of the Chicago School. He advocated original American architecture and designed the famous Rookery (1885–88) and Monadnock (1889–92) buildings. He felt architecture should reflect its era and environment. "It springs from the past, but is not tied to it."[12]

Root was often referred to as brilliant; he was an excellent draftsman, musician, and writer with a wonderful sense of humor. When the cornerstone of the Woman's Christian Temperance Union building was being laid in 1890, the assembled group stood through a number of long speeches. When they were completed, John Root turned to the group of businessmen and said, "Let's go and get a drink!"[13]

In 1873 Daniel Burnham and John Wellborn Root became partners. Their practice was launched in 1874 when they received the commission to design John Sherman's house on Prairie Avenue, the most exclusive neighborhood at the time. Sherman was one of the founders of the Union Stockyards.

The highlight of their work together was the Columbian Exposition of 1893 with Daniel Burnham as chief in charge of construction and John Root as his consulting partner. It was Root's idea to attract the leading architects of the day to design the buildings for the Columbian Exposition. Frederick Law Olmsted and Root were responsible for choosing Jackson Park as the site for the Fair. Root sketched a number of buildings of different styles and colors in advance of the Fair. He wanted to offer proof of new ideas for the Exposition buildings.

However, one cold January night in 1891, John Root hosted a reception at his home on Astor Street for the architects visiting Chicago to plan the Columbian Exposition. After the meeting, he escorted his guests to their carriages outside his home, and he caught pneumonia. He died four days later at the young age of 41, and the world lost an outstanding architect. "My father never got over the shock of it," said Burnham's son.[14] Root's vision of the general layout of the Fair was praised by Halsey Ives (director of Fine Arts), "The real art work – the design – was the ensemble."[15]

After Root's death, 1310 North Astor continued to be occupied by his wife, children, and sister-in-law, Harriet Monroe, poet and founder of *Poetry Magazine*. Thirty-two year old Harriet had noticed that poetry was being overlooked for the Dedication Ceremony of the Exposition and this seemed to her "unjust and ill-advised."[16] She approached the committee and suggested they hire her to write a poem entitled *Columbian Ode* to be read at the opening ceremonies. The poem was too long and not well-received by the committee. She did condense it, and delivered it to the committee with a bill for $1,000. The committee decided to pay the bill and give the poem to the Board of Lady Managers headed by Mrs. Potter Palmer.

Mrs. Palmer rejected the poem, insisting the board did not commission the poem and it was not representative of woman's work. In the end, the poem was read by an actress at the Dedication Ceremony of the Columbian Exposition in Manufacturer's Hall. The Hall was thirty-two acres long. As it was before the invention of the microphone, very few people heard it!

Copies of the poem were sold at the Fair for $.25, but, to the chagrin of Ms. Monroe, it did not receive much attention. Most of the 5000 copies were used for fuel that winter. The New York *World* had published the poem in advance of the Fair without Monroe's permission. She sued the newspaper and was awarded $5,000![17]

The neighborhood continued to grow in importance until post World War II when owners found it difficult to keep up their homes without the help of servants. Many homes were turned into apartments. The 1960s and 70s were the tear-down years. Landmark preservation was a term not understood or of interest to most people. In February of 1967, author M. Williams of the *Daily News* wrote that Astor Street could never be an historic site – Lincoln never slept here – and except

Harriet Monroe, John Root's sister-in-law, was a poet and founder of
Poetry Magazine. *(Chicago History Museum)*

for Mrs. Waller's house (Charnley House) there are no real architectural monuments.(!)

When architect Bertrand Goldberg (designer of Marina Towers apartment building) who lived in the 1500 block of Astor Street was interviewed by the *Chicago Tribune Magazine* in 1973, he said about high-rises in the neighborhood, "I don't know what they have done except destroy the environment that gave Astor Street its value."

By the 1980s, many of the homes that had been divided into apartments returned to single family residences and today the neighborhood reflects an ever-changing city.

Mrs. Palmer in a stunning winter embroidered dress with matching jacket and hat, likely designed by Worth. (Courtesy of Pauline Wood Egan)

Chapter 5

LEADING
THE PROCESSION

Mrs. Bates, Mrs. Palmer's literary name in Henry Fuller's novel
With the Procession *said, "People in our position would naturally*
be expected to have a Corot." After her death it was discovered
that her Corot of the Girl with the Lute *was a copy.*
Silhouette in Diamonds
by Ishbel Ross, page 156

ALTHOUGH BERTHA PALMER never received any formal training in art, she always had an interest and collecting art became an important pursuit, befitting her acknowledged position as the "Queen" of Chicago society. The castle had been built by 1885, now it was time to fill it.

Mrs. Palmer was a founding member and board member of the Chicago Society of Decorative Arts, a purchasing affiliate, which changed its name in 1889 to the Antiquarian Society of the Art Institute. Women became actively involved in the Art Institute through these societies, buying artists' works and donating them to the museum.

There were some negative comments about the new name of Antiquarian Society and one woman declined membership because she was "not old enough!"[1]

The Palmers had purchased Tang figurines, Chinese porcelain, jade (although Mrs. Palmer never thought Americans appreciated her collection), paintings from the Romantic and Barbizon schools, and more contemporary paintings during their trips abroad. But the bulk of their art collection was purchased in 1891–92 when Mrs. Palmer traveled to Paris as Chairman of the Board of the Lady Managers for the Columbian Exposition of 1893.

Bust of Bertha Palmer, sculpted by Rodin, in the Rodin Museum, Paris.
(Courtesy of Mr. William Locke)

The ninety-foot-long combination ballroom and picture gallery was designed by Henry Hardenbergh and added in 1893 to house Mrs. Palmer's enormous art collection. (Chicago History Museum)

Sarah Hallowell, the Palmers' art advisor, had lived in Chicago, and worked with Potter Palmer when she had served as secretary of the art department of the Inter-State Industrial Exposition. The Exposition building, made of wood, brick and glass and designed by W.W. Boyington (who also designed the Water Tower on Michigan Avenue), was erected in 1873 to serve as a center for music, art, commerce, and industry. The building, sometimes referred to as the "Crystal Palace," was the site of summer concerts led by Theodore Thomas in 1879, the exciting Republican Convention of 1880, and art exhibits organized by Hallowell. Hallowell displayed a large number of contemporary paintings at the Exposition, including works by Monet, Pissarro and Degas in 1890, three years before the Columbian Exposition.[2] The building was razed in 1892 to make way for the structure that hosted the World Congresses during the Columbian Exposition and which became the Art Institute at the close of the Fair.

As the Palmers' art agent, Hallowell introduced them to Paul Durand Ruel, the Impressionist art dealer (and agent for Monet, Manet, Renoir and later Cassatt) and to Mary Cassatt. Both Ruel and Cassatt were living in France and promoting the Impressionist painters. Although

Degas sculpture purchased by Bertha Palmer. (Courtesy of Mr. Arthur Wood)

Mrs. Palmer actively sought Hallowell's advice about talent and purchases, she also based her choices on personal appeal and her husband's opinion. Potter Palmer was also active in helping Charles Hutchinson (President of the Art Institute) and Martin Ryerson (one of the most important donors to the Art Institute) by scouting out paintings during his travels to Europe.[3] Ryerson and Hutchinson were always hunting for new acquisitions for the Art Institute, and because of their shrewdness in the face of an economic panic of 1893–4, they purchased twenty-one paintings from the Demidoff collection of Old Masters in Italy. Today one single painting in the collection is more valuable than the total amount paid.[4]

Charles Hutchinson said that "no collection of paintings is valuable until the collector has sent some to the attic."[5]

> *"In collecting you always have to have a leader*
> *and Mrs. Palmer was prescient enough to realize that they*
> *(the Impressionists) would catch on."*
> Director of the Art Institute, Daniel Catton Rich
> *Silhouette in Diamonds*
> by Ishbel Ross, page 147

Mrs. Palmer's first Impressionist painting was *On the Stage* by Degas, purchased in 1889 for $500. Three years later she purchased another painting by Degas, *Dancers Preparing for the Ballet,* but she became particularly fond of paintings by Monet. She purchased seven by Monet in 1891 and an additional twenty-two in 1892, enough to make a frieze around the walls of her picture gallery, which had been added in 1893 to house her newly acquired art treasures.[6] At one time

According to architect and historian Thomas E. Tallmadge, the Potter Palmer castle was an American architect's idea of what a baronial castle should be. (Chicago History Museum)

she owned as many as ninety Monet paintings, most of them painted during the 1890s.[7]

In 1891 she met Degas, Pisarro, and visited Monet at Giverny, and spoke with them in flawless French. She also purchased four Sisleys, eleven Renoirs, and six Pisarros, among others, in 1892, a big purchasing year. This was an exciting time to travel, to meet the artists and to know for certain that the painting purchased was genuine.[8]

That same year she purchased two prized Renoir paintings: *The Canoeist's Luncheon* (also referred to as *The Rower's Lunch*) and her favorite painting *Dans le Cirque* painted in 1879 and costing $1750. The painting of two circus girls, a study in yellow tones, originally hung in the foyer of the infamous Moulin Rouge in Paris. The girls performed on the trapeze and received the oranges laying at their feet for compensation. Because *Dans le Cirque* provided so much enjoyment to Mrs. Palmer, the painting hung for some time in her bedroom. After

Potter Palmer died and she was living in Europe, the painting always accompanied her.[9]

Stacks of Wheat at the End of Summer was one of fifteen studies of the same subject that were painted by Monet and first displayed at Durand-Ruel's gallery in Paris in 1891. Mrs. Palmer attended the exhibition and purchased eight of the fifteen from the artist and art dealer, making her the first collector to understand the significance of the series, and in turn introduce the concept to Chicago. The series of haystacks started on a late summer evening and ended on a winter day. Mrs. Palmer preferred the color and light of the summer and autumn scenes rather than the colder winter scenes that Monet favored.

It is difficult to determine which fifteen were in the original exhibition because Monet painted so many (thirty survive today), but we do know that Mrs. Palmer owned three (of eight purchased) from the 1891 exhibition. Later Mrs. Palmer purchased a ninth haystack from a private owner. For a time the series could "breathe contentedly" as Pissarro said when the paintings were first displayed as a group in Durand-Ruel's gallery.[10] Within three years Mrs. Palmer sold three of the paintings, acting as a dealer, a role she often chose – buying and selling paintings at a profit. After 1890, her art collection was in a constant state of change.

In 1892, Mrs. Palmer visited Mary Cassatt in Paris to commission her to paint a large mural to be entitled "Modern Woman" for the Woman's Building at the Columbian Exposition of 1893. This was the last step in securing artists for the decoration of the Woman's building. Mrs. Palmer's first choice, Elizabeth Gardner, a better known artist, had declined the invitation because of the amount of physical work involved.[11] There were to be two murals, one at either end of the Woman's Building, and Mary Fairchild MacMonnies, wife of the famous Exposition sculptor, had accepted the commission for "Primitive Woman."

Forty-eight year old Cassatt was an American woman of exceptional talent living in France in order to pursue her art. She wrote to art agent and friend Sarah Hallowell, "After all give me France – women do not have to fight for recognition here, if they do serious work."[12]

Cassatt, a good friend of Degas, was relatively unknown in the United States. Degas, who said about Cassatt, "No woman has the right to draw like that" was strongly against Cassatt's accepting the commission as it was such a departure from her easel work. Cassatt agreed to paint the mural because she thought it would be interesting to work on

The Mary Cassatt mural, entitled "Modern Woman" was mounted at the top of the end wall in the Woman's Building. (Chicago History Museum)

The Palace of Fine Arts was designed by Charles Atwood and contained valuable paintings during the Columbian Exposition. Today it is the Museum of Science and Industry. (Chicago History Museum)

something new, although the thought of the time and the physical exertion required caused her some worry.[13]

At this time, Mrs. Palmer purchased a set of Mary Cassatt's color prints and bought a Cassatt mother-and-child painting from art dealer Durand-Ruel. The 12 x 58 foot pictorial mural painted with rich, bright colors (Giotto was her model) illustrated young women plucking the fruits of knowledge from trees and pursuing fame. It was hung at the end of the Woman's gallery, higher than Cassatt would have liked. In a letter written to Mrs. Palmer in October of 1892, Cassatt wrote that she thought Mrs. Palmer would be pleased with her work, but maybe not appreciate it as much if it is "dragged up forty-eight feet!"[14]

But Mary Cassatt never attended the Columbian Exposition to view the mural which received less than enthusiastic reviews, and although she barely broke even financially, it was not a complete loss. Cassatt used the models and garden setting for theme-related paintings that were part of a large show that opened in late 1893 in Durand-Ruel's gallery in Paris.[15] Unfortunately, the mural painted by Cassatt was lost at the close of the Fair.

Because the 1890 art exhibit at the Exposition building had been extremely successful with art critics and the general public, Sarah Hallowell was recommended for head of the art department for the Columbian Exposition. There was just one problem: the committee wanted a man. Although Mrs. Palmer actively promoted Hallowell for the job, she was instead given the responsibility to secure "Foreign Masterpieces Owned by Americans" for the loan exhibition housed in the Palace of Fine Arts. Designed by Charles Atwood, the arts building was constructed with a brick substructure under the plaster because it was to contain valuable works of art. According to renowned sculptor Augustus Saint-Gaudens, the Palace of Fine Arts was the "best thing since the Parthenon."[16]

The official French show at the Exposition contained only one French Impressionist painting because the French nation had not yet acknowledged the "native geniuses,"[17] but Hallowell's Loan Collection contained 126 paintings, mostly French.[18] Many prominent Americans such as Cornelius Vanderbilt, Jay Gould, William Crocker, H.O. Havemeyers, Alexander Cassatt (Mary Cassatt's brother), and the Potter Palmers donated their paintings. As a result, the best works of art displayed at the Fair were found in the Fine Arts Building.[19]

The Impressionist paintings caused quite a stir among the visitors, many of whom had never viewed impressionism, and words such as "sketchy," "garish," and "blotchy" were used to describe them.[20] But the majority of the works presented were more conservative. The favorites were Hovenden's *Breaking the Home Ties* and Breton's *Song of the Lark*, which are still popular today.

Initially Mrs. Palmer did not want to participate in the Loan Exhibit during a time in which she described herself as the "nation's hostess and the nation's head woman servant."[21] She was entertaining on a regular basis and wished to keep her art collection intact, displayed in the ballroom of her castle. Sarah Hallowell appealed to Potter Palmer, and they consented to lend fifteen paintings to the exhibit.

When the fair closed in October of 1893 the pure Greek classic style Palace of Fine Arts became the Columbian Museum that evolved into the Field Museum of Natural History. When the Field Museum opened a new building in 1920, the former Art Palace was left vacant. The Commercial Club of Chicago, founded in 1877 by a group of civic-minded businessmen involved in Chicago's development, was interested in opening a science museum. Club member Julius Rosenwald, philanthropist and president of Sears Roebuck & Company, pledged $3,000,000 (which eventually became $5,000,000) to convert the Palace of Fine Arts into a science museum. The museum organization was established in 1926, and Rosenwald asked that his name not appear on the building, thus displaying a sense of modesty very rare today.

For a short time it was referred to as the Rosenwald Industrial Museum, but it became the Museum of Science and Industry in 1928 and remains so today. Architect Charles Atwood, who was comparatively unknown before the Exposition, designed the only building from the Columbian Exposition that remains in Jackson Park today.

Mrs. Palmer in a Worth gown of cut silk velvet. (Courtesy of Pauline Wood Egan)

COLUMBIAN EXPOSITION

*"Even more important than the discovery of Columbus,
which we are gathered here to celebrate, is the fact that
the General Government has just discovered woman."*
Bertha Honoré Palmer's speech at the opening ceremonies
of the Columbian Exposition, October 12, 1892.
Chicago History, Spring 1977, page 23

UNFORTUNATELY, MOST PEOPLE never heard this speech in
the Manufacturers Building that covered thirty-two acres because loud
speakers had not been invented.[1] They might have read about it in one
of the twenty-nine daily newspapers in print in 1892!

In 1890, Chicago won the bid to host the World's Columbian
Exposition, but not without resistance from New York City. When the
race was tied between the two cities, the *New York Sun* printed, "Pay
no attention to the nonsensical claims of that windy city. Its people
couldn't build a World's Fair if they won it."[2]

But Chicago's efforts proved successful in April of 1890 when
President Harrison signed the bill for Chicago to sponsor the 400th anniversary of Columbus' voyage to America. The date was pushed ahead one
year to 1893 to give the city additional planning time to present a "jumbo"
event.[3] Talk of surpassing the Paris Exhibition of 1889, which had introduced the Eiffel Tower, dominated the minds of Chicagoans.

The financing of the Fair was an important issue in the competition. Chicago had quickly secured over $5,000,000 in public pledges to
cover the cost of the Fair, with Marshall Field as the biggest subscriber
for stock in the Fair.[4] Ward Allister, social arbiter of New York and good
friend of Mrs. Astor, commented on Chicago's hosting the Columbian
Exposition: "The contact of New York and Chicago society during the

Daniel Burnham and John Root in their office in the Rookery Building during planning of the Columbian Exposition. (Chicago History Museum)

World's Fair cannot help but open the eyes of our Western natives to our superiority."[5]

By 1890, Chicago was the fastest spreading city in America, with the largest cable-car system in the world. Over 1000 trains a day were coming in and out of Chicago on the Illinois Central, but it was also a city that continued to be plagued by strikes, culminating in the Pullman strike of 1894, when the National Guard was called in for assistance.

Chicago lacked an adequate sewer system, and as a result, typhoid and cholera killed over two thousand residents a year. The Great Sanitary and Ship Canal that ultimately cleaned Chicago's waters was not completed until 1900, well after the Columbian Exposition.[6]

Chicago won the bid to host the Columbian Exposition to celebrate the 400th anniversary of Columbus' voyage to America. (Chicago History Museum)

In the early 1890s, the *Chicago Tribune* started printing articles about economic turbulence in the markets. People were afraid of a full-blown Panic. But the "Gay Nineties" was also a time of growth and expansion in Chicago, with many ethnic neighborhoods that encompassed a variety of cultures and languages.[7] A feeling of optimism permeated the city as Chicago prepared to host its first World's Fair and show the world its glorious and prosperous city as its main exhibit.[8]

Daniel Burnham was selected as chief in charge of construction, his architectural partner John Root as designer-in-chief (replaced by Charles Atwood after Root's sudden death), Frederick Law Olmsted (already well-known professionally for designing Central Park) and Harry Codman were selected as landscape architects, and Mrs. Potter Palmer as Chairman of the Board of Lady Managers.

Burnham famously said: "Make no little plans. They have no magic to stir men's blood."

Burnham hired the leading architects of the day to design the buildings for the Exposition, initially eliminating Chicago architects. The resulting criticism from Chicago architects and some leading citizens, including Potter Palmer, changed Burnham's mind, and he added Adler & Sullivan, Burling & Whitehouse, Jenney & Mundie, S.S. Beman, and Henry Ives Cobb.[9]

All the architects met in Chicago in January of 1891 to plan for the Columbian Exposition. One cold blustery day they traveled to Jackson Park to view the dreary exposition site.

A Boston architect asked Daniel Burnham, "Do you mean to say that you really propose opening a Fair here by '93?"

"Yes," replied Burnham, "we intend to."

"It can't be done," said the Bostonian.

"That point," retorted Burnham, "is settled."[10]

The architects decided upon a classical style of architecture promoted by Charles F. McKim, and a common cornice line to give harmony to the buildings surrounding the lagoon and Grand Basin.

After the meeting of the architects, Augustus Saint-Gaudens, well-known sculptor and supervisor of all sculpture at the Exposition said, "Do you realize that this is the greatest meeting of artists since the fifteenth century?"[11]

Burnham, along with Mayor Carter Harrison, hired a police force of 2,000 men, called the Columbian Guard, to patrol the 600-acre site. Popular Mayor Carter Harrison, serving his fifth term, was a great showman and proponent of the Fair. He fought against efforts to close the Fair on Sundays and kept a watch for any disorder. However, years later a story surfaced that a police inspector had sold a "pickpocket monopoly" to two men, but they had been restricted to a measly $100 a day.[12]

Jane Addams of Hull House was one of the attendees who had her purse snatched, but an officer of the Columbian Guard retrieved it.[13]

Harrison always said, "You can't legislate morality."[14]

William Pretyman, director of color for the Exposition, wanted a variety of colors for the buildings, the same idea as his friend, Root, who had sketched different architectural styles and colors prior to his death. Burnham insisted on a uniform white or off-white for the Court of Honor and Pretyman resigned. The complexion of the architecture of the Fair and "White City" might have been vastly different had John Root lived and his ideas been supported by Pretyman, Louis Sullivan, and Henry Ives Cobb (who broke with the classical style) for the use of color and Chicago style architecture.[15]

Prior to the Fair, the city and American architecture had been largely Romanesque in style, but the classical style prevailed after the Fair. According to Louis Sullivan, "Architecture died in the land of the free and home of the brave. The damage wrought by the World's Fair will last for half a century from its date, if not longer."[16]

A Scribner's *cover story on
the Columbian Exposition.*
(Chicago History Museum)

*The bicycle craze swept the country
in the 1890s. Women were able to
escape from their families to bike the
neighboring streets.*

But many believed the magic of the architecture of the "White City" captivated the audience who attended the Fair. William Le Baron Jenney, father of the Chicago skyscraper, argued, "The lessons taught by the architecture of the World's Fair are valuable and will improve the architecture of Chicago."[17]

After John Root's death, Burnham hired Charles Atwood to assume Root's duties, and with his increased responsibilities continued preparations for the Fair, incorporating a filter system for the drinking water and lighting the grounds with electricity. For many visitors, this was the first time they had seen electricity.

Burnham spent almost all of his time inspecting the Fair grounds. "Often," his son said, "he would take us children, too, and let us sleep in his cabin on the Wooded Island. After ten o'clock at night we had the whole island to ourselves."[18]

The major Fair buildings were constructed to be temporary fixtures in Jackson Park, framed with iron or steel, covered with a mixture of plaster, cement and hemp, and finally white-washed with a hose instead of a brush as suggested by Frank Millet, the new "Director of Color" and a well respected artist.[19]

Favored travel to the exposition was by Yerkes' electric cable car introduced in 1890, boat ride along Lake Michigan, Illinois Central Railway, elevated train or by bicycle. The bicycle craze swept the country in the 1890s. There were over 500 bicycle clubs in Chicago at the time of the Columbian Exposition, and bicycling became a very popular means of transportation around the Fair Grounds. New bicycles cost as much as $150 at a time when the average salary per year was between $200 and $400.[20]

Thanks to this new fad, as well as women entering the workforce as operators of the telephone and typewriter, fashions were becoming more modern and liberating. Women were able to wear culottes and escape from their families to bike the neighborhood streets. But one woman donned a flesh-colored sweater and black tights to ride her bicycle in the busy traffic of Dearborn Street. She was arrested for disorderly conduct and fined $25.[21]

The "Gibson Girl" look (created by illustrator Charles Gibson) included a skirt, blouse, and jacket, but the up-to-date outfit still required a corset and petticoats.

The Act of Congress that created the World's Columbian Exposition included a Board of Lady Managers. Mrs. Potter Palmer was selected as Chairman with a board of 117 women chosen from every state and territory, members-at-large, and nine from the city of Chicago. Mrs. Palmer wrote: "There has been much unfavorable comment upon the somewhat ridiculous title of the Board, and with justice, but the fault is not with the women. Its membership comprises as many representative workers in the active industries of the country as if it were composed of men."[22]

Mrs. Palmer traveled to Washington, D.C. to appear before the Appropriations Committee. She sought to secure money for a Woman's Building to exhibit women's industries over the centuries. Mrs. Palmer brought together women from forty-one nations to display the largest quantity of work at a national exhibition. Needlework arts experienced a re-birth at the Fair and, as a result, many impoverished women from Europe sold their embroideries and lace. But the committee could not accept all donations. They had to turn away the female embalmer who wanted to exhibit a corpse![23]

Maud Howe Elliot wrote in her book *Art and Handicraft in the Woman's Building* (the first copy presented to Mrs. Palmer) and published in 1893 that the most significant contribution of the Woman's Building was the bringing together of women from the most distant parts

The Administration Building of the Columbian Exposition was designed by the famous architect of the day, Richard Morris Hunt. (Chicago History Museum)

Sophia Hayden, the first woman to graduate from MIT's School of Architecture, won the competition to design the Woman's Building. (Chicago History Museum)

of the land. There were constant battles with the Isabellas, women board members who were all suffragists and had their own agenda. At this time, Wyoming was the only state in which women had the right to vote.[24]

Susan B. Anthony, nearly seventy years old and the veteran leader of women suffragists, played an important role in organizing women to be part of the management of the 1893 Fair. She chose to work behind the scenes because so many of the officials were antagonistic towards the suffragists.

Mrs. Palmer traveled throughout Europe to solicit donations for exhibit in the Woman's Building. A beautifully dressed woman with grace, style, and brains representing Chicago was an oddity to most people. Her role as the city's diplomat proved beneficial to Chicago, which had been labeled a "cow town" for many years. Not only did she travel abroad, but she also asked board members to "scour the countryside" for women's work.[25] Mrs. Palmer contacted the patent office in Washington, D.C. to include inventions by women. Although there were 3000 patents on file by women, an odd assortment of items was displayed: a combination sofa and bathtub, a dress stand that could become a fire escape, and the Hambell egg and cake beater that received 60,000 orders. One of the best inventions, the dish-washer, was not on exhibit, but it was being used in the restaurants located on the Fair Grounds. Ellen Henrotin, an active Chicago philanthropist, was disappointed that none of the most valuable scientific inventions were shown.[26]

Daniel Burnham selected Richard Morris Hunt, one of the leading architects of the day and responsible for designing the Administration Building, to design the Woman's Building. But the Board of Lady Managers decided to hold a competition in February of 1891 to hire a woman architect.

Twenty-one year old Sophia Hayden, the first woman graduate of the architectural school of MIT, won the competition and traveled to Chicago to meet with Mrs. Palmer. Hayden thought she had control over the interior of the building as well as the design and started declining donations that she said would make the interior a "hodge-podge" of items. The donations included columns, balustrades, and a carved wooden door![27]

Mrs. Palmer was determined to accept as many donations as possible and hired Candace Wheeler, a well-known New York decorator, to complete the task. Ms. Hayden had a nervous breakdown in Daniel Burnham's office and reportedly never designed another building.[28]

The 265-foot tall Ferris Wheel on the Midway Plaisance at the 1893 World's Columbian Exposition. CHS, ICHi-21713.

The fifty-cent ride on the Ferris Wheel proved to be one of the highlights of the Fair. (Chicago History Museum)

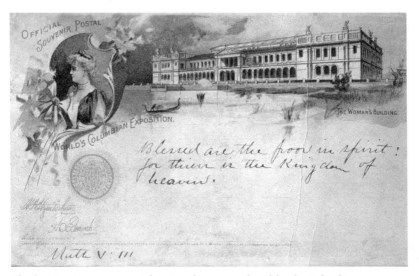

The first American commercial postcards were produced for the Columbian Exposition. The Women's Building and Mrs. Potter Palmer postcards have become collector's items. (Collection of Sally S. Kalmbach)

The Woman's Building was one of the first buildings started and completed at the Fair, but covering less than two acres, it was considerably smaller than the buildings in the Court of Honor. The Café on the rooftop of the Woman's Building, which was a last minute idea initiated by the lady managers, was reportedly the best restaurant at the Fair and most successful financially. Mrs. Riley, who ran the concession, made a profit of $44,000![29]

The midway, called the "playground of all nations," housed the famous Ferris Wheel designed by George Ferris. The fifty cent ride on the wheel carrying 1440 people up to a height of 250 feet proved to be one of the highlights of the Fair.[30] What happened to the Ferris Wheel? After its success at the Exposition it was moved to Clark and Wrightwood Streets to be part of an entertainment center, but the crowds never came. It had one swan song at the St. Louis Fair of 1904 and then became scrap at a construction site. George Ferris died in 1896 at the age of thirty-seven, so he never learned the fate of his famous wheel.

The Midway, flanked by buildings of the newly opened University of Chicago, contained every activity imaginable with native families from Africa, South Sea Islands, Eskimos (who suffered from Chicago's

The State of New York offered its beautiful pavilion, designed by McKim, Mead and White, as a permanent Woman's Memorial Building, but the authorities refused the Board's request to allow the building to remain in Jackson Park. (Chicago History Museum)

summer heat), and other exotic locales. It was a kaleidoscope of activity, ever-changing throughout the Fair grounds. The big question: Would you ever be able to see it all?[31] Mrs. Addie Hibbard Gregory took her young daughters to the Fair every Saturday for six months. When Mrs. Gregory finished one of her lectures about architecture, a visitor said to her daughter, "Well, little girl, your mother is going to get you educated." "Yes," the child replied, "but I don't know if I will live through it!"[32]

Three days before the closing of the Fair on October 28th, Mayor Carter Harrison received a visitor at his southern colonial style home on Ashland Avenue. A young disgruntled man named Prendergast, who had failed to gain a position in Harrison's administration, shot and killed the mayor in his front hallway. The killer was declared insane because he was not qualified for any city job. Many years later Chicago newspaper writer Ben Hecht (who became a celebrated screenwriter) wrote, "Most of the people who held office in Chicago were feeble-minded, crazy or dishonest – and most all were and are unfit for public office – so labeling Prendergast mad for seeking a city position he wasn't fitted for was a poor farce of an excuse. Whoever was fit in Chicago's highest offices?"[33]

Carter Harrison's death was a tragedy for his family and the city. All the closing ceremonies of the Fair were cancelled, and a funeral was held instead.

The Fair was immortalized in a variety of ways. The first American commercial postcards were produced for the Columbian Exposition, and postcards of the Woman's Building and Mrs. Potter Palmer became popular collector items. Charles Arnold, official Fair photographer, produced a large number of photos that were turned into souvenir booklets. The "spoon" mania was at its height, and the Woman's Building was re-produced on at least fifteen different spoon designs.

Journalists from around the world traveled to the Fair and wrote articles about the exposition that appeared in newspapers, magazines, and journals. In the 1960s a series of articles about the Fair that had been written by Marian Shaw were found at a Minneapolis rummage sale. Shaw had spent several weeks at the Fair and wrote her impressions, which included the Woman's Building. She lauded the rapid advancement made by women during the past hundred years, as illustrated in the Woman's Building. Her one criticism: the exhibit displays were too crowded. Maybe Sophia Hayden, designer of the Woman's Pavilion, had been correct![34]

In October of 1893, at the close of the Fair, a permanent Woman's Memorial Building was proposed by the ladies to act as a museum with many items included from the Exposition. The state of New York offered its beautiful pavilion designed by McKim, Mead, and White, but the authorities refused the Board's request that the building be allowed to remain in Jackson Park. Mrs. Palmer was not interested in tackling the job and the economy had continued to suffer, so the idea was abandoned.

At the close of the Fair the Lady Managers presented Mrs. Palmer with her portrait painted by the Swedish artist Anders Zorn in appreciation for the work she had done as President. Mrs. Palmer's efforts to help improve women's education, working conditions and wages were best served in her position as Chairman of the Board of Lady Managers for the Columbian Exposition.

In Mrs. Palmer's closing speech to the Lady Managers she acknowledged that employment of women was a foregone conclusion, but women worked in the main because of the incompetence of men, the natural providers. If men would assume their responsibilities, women could stay home and tend to their "higher service."[35]

The Columbian Exposition illustrated Chicago's energy and spirit last displayed on such a grand scale in the re-building of the city after the Fire of 1871. The juxtaposition of the "White City" with the rest of the city gave hope and a vision to Daniel Burnham and others of what a city could be in the future. Burnham's experience designing the Exposition paved the way for his future as a city planner, resulting in the Burnham Plan of 1909 for the city of Chicago.

Mrs. Palmer in one of her traveling suits, photographed by M. J. Steffens, a prominent Chicago photographer who took the majority of the studio portraits of the Palmer family. This copy, autographed by Mrs. Palmer, reads: "Most Sincerely Yours, Bertha Honoré Palmer, March 1900" (Courtesy of Pauline Wood Egan)

THE END OF
THE PROCESSION

$\mathcal{T}$HE FAIR WAS over, Bertha Palmer was tired, and the Palmers departed for a world tour to rest and visit with some of the people whom Mrs. Palmer had met during her days as Chairman of the Board of Lady Managers. Still in her forties, Mrs. Palmer was full of energy and ready to tackle the diplomatic world. She campaigned for her husband to become U.S. Ambassador to Germany. Although friendly with both President Cleveland and Vice-President Adlai Stevenson, this was one race she did not win. Mr. Palmer, who had always shied away from any political post, was probably relieved.[1]

Newport society had always fascinated her, so by the late 1890s Mrs. Palmer decided to make this her new conquest. She rented a house, hosted a dance for her niece Julia Grant, the former president's granddaughter, and entertained royalty traveling to the United States whom she knew from her Columbian Exposition days. Always the pioneer and adventurer, she was seeking that next step to experience life.

In 1900, President McKinley appointed her as the only woman to the National Commission at the Paris Exposition, along with Ferdinand Peck from Chicago, who was one of the primary organizers for the building of the Auditorium Theater.

Mrs. Palmer helped secure places for women on the awards juries (something she was unsuccessful in obtaining during the Columbian Exposition) and more women representation in the Congresses, and she was instrumental in the appointment of Jane Addams to the Department of Philanthropy. Afterward she was awarded the French Legion Medal of Honor.

By the turn of the century, Potter Palmer's health started to deteriorate, and after he died in 1902, Mrs. Palmer moved to London and entered the Marlborough Circle of Edward VII. England had been through years of mourning with Queen Victoria, and the country was

In 1900, President McKinley appointed Bertha Palmer to the National Commission at the Paris Exposition, where she wore this dress and slip. (Courtesy of Timothy Long, Costume Curator, Chicago History Museum)

ready for a more entertaining ruler. Mrs. Palmer rented a house on Carlton Square and dined regularly with the king.

Mrs. Palmer ceased purchasing paintings during her years abroad, but continued to collect sculpture, furniture, and other works of art.[2]

In 1910 she purchased vast amounts of land in Sarasota, Florida, and was able to pursue gardening, a favorite hobby. She raised oranges, vegetables, and livestock, all of which appealed to her business sense. The circle that had begun at Potter's Field in Albany County ended in Sarasota, Florida, with Mrs. Palmer turning in her Worth gowns and diamond tiara to return to the land. But periodically she would return to Chicago to host the Charity Ball.

As late as May 1, 1918, she had expressed every intention of returning to Chicago to help with the war effort, but died in Sarasota on May 5. When the *Herald Tribune* received notice of her death, they printed the best response: "There can be no grief at the end of such a journey."

Mrs. Palmer's will stipulated that her sons, Honoré and Potter, Jr., select paintings from her collection valued at $100,000 to be donated to the Art Institute of Chicago. This group of fifty-two paintings was presented to the Institute in 1922 and became part of the Potter Palmer collection.[3] The collection included a large number of Impressionist

Crowds gathered in front of the Palmer "castle" in May of 1918 to mourn the passing of Mrs. Potter Palmer. (Chicago History Museum)

paintings, two Delacroix, Millet's *Rail Splitter,* and four Cazins. Years later, a visitor to the Art Institute remarked that the gallery of Renoirs must have cost the museum a fortune. The president of the Institute said, "Not at all. In Chicago, we don't buy Renoirs. We inherit them from our grandmothers."[4]

The Lake Shore Drive castle and all its contents went to Honoré and Potter, Jr. and Potter decided to buy his brother's interest and make it his home. Several years later, in 1928, the Palmers sold the castle to Vincent Bendix, of Bendix Corporation. Rumors circulated about the fate of the famous castle. Reportedly Mr. Bendix hoped to use it as a guest house where he could entertain his friends and house his own art collection, but his dream was never realized. The castle finally reverted to the Palmer family in 1933, was used by the Red Cross during World War II, and was razed in 1950.

The destruction of the Palmer castle marked the end to a more gracious era, when Mrs. Palmer reigned as Chicago's queen for almost thirty years. She had been instrumental in helping women improve their lives, from the establishment of the first juvenile court to helping the milliners form their first union.

View of the "castle" looking south. (Chicago History Museum)

The Columbian Exposition was a turning point in women's lives. They achieved a new status on the road to financial and social independence. The organizational and managerial skills demonstrated in the running of the Woman's Building by the Board of Lady Managers provided a boost for the suffragists and paved the way for women entering the work force in greater numbers.

Mrs. Palmer was urged, and rightfully so, to give the dedication speech at the Columbian Exposition because the women felt she stood for the "Queen of Time and Womankind of the World."[5]

APPENDIX

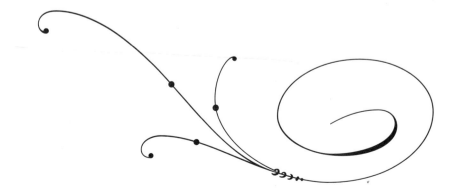

TIME LINE

1837

Chicago incorporated
as a city

1850s

Potter Palmer and the
Honoré family settle
in Chicago

1870

Bertha Honoré and
Potter Palmer marry

1882

First house built along
Lake Shore Drive

1885

Potter Palmer castle
completed on
Lake Shore Drive

1891

Charnley House on
Astor Street designed
by Louis Sullivan

1902–10

Mrs. Palmer travels
and lives in England
and France

1910

Mrs. Palmer purchases
vast amounts of land
in Sarasota, Florida

1918

Mrs. Palmer dies

1871

First Palmer House completed (September)

Great Chicago Fire (October)

1874–75

Second Palmer House completed and Palmers move into their quarters

1880

Cardinal's Residence built in the Gold Coast

Potter Palmer purchases land to develop the Gold Coast

1893

Columbian Exposition held in Chicago

1900

Mrs. Palmer attends the Paris Exhibition as a member of the National Commission appointed by President McKinley

1902

Potter Palmer dies

1922

Fifty-two paintings donated to the Art Institute of Chicago as part of the Potter Palmer collection

ENDNOTES

CHAPTER 1

1. Ross, Ishbel. *Silhouette In Diamonds – The Life of Mrs. Potter Palmer* (New York: Harper & Brothers, Publishers, 1960), 32.

2. Ross, Ishbel. *Silhouette In Diamonds – The Life of Mrs. Potter Palmer* (New York: Harper & Brothers, Publishers, 1960), 30.

3. Martin, Ralph G. *Cissy: The Extraordinary Life of Eleanor Medill Patterson* (New York: Simon & Schuster, 1979), 27.

4. Ross, Ishbel. *Silhouette In Diamonds – The Life of Mrs. Potter Palmer* (New York: Harper & Brothers, Publishers, 1960), 10.

5. Miller, Donald L. *City of the Century: The Epic of Chicago and the Making of America* (New York: Simon & Schuster, 1996), 140.

6. Ross, Ishbel. *Silhouette In Diamonds – The Life of Mrs. Potter Palmer* (New York: Harper & Brothers, Publishers, 1960), 17.

7. Poole, Ernest. *Giants Gone – Men Who Made Chicago* (New York: McGraw-Hill Book Company, 1943), 120.

8. Ross, Ishbel. *Silhouette In Diamonds – The Life of Mrs. Potter Palmer* (New York: Harper & Brothers, Publishers, 1960), 26.

9. Poole, Ernest. *Giants Gone – Men Who Made Chicago* (New York: McGraw-Hill Book Company, 1943), 101.

10. Lewis, Lloyd and Smith, Henry Justin. *Chicago, The History of Its Reputation* (New York: Harcourt, Brace and Company, 1929), 288.

11. Ross, Ishbel. *Silhouette In Diamonds – The Life of Mrs. Potter Palmer* (New York: Harper & Brothers, Publishers, 1960), 8.

12. This story was told to me by Potter Palmer IV. Per discussion June 2003.

13. Furer, Howard B., ed. *Chicago: A Chronological & Documentary History, 1784–1970* (Dobbs Ferry, NY: Oceana Publications, 1974), 20.

14. Longstreet, Stephen. *Chicago 1860–1919* (New York: David McKay Company, Inc., 1973), 103.

15. Masters, Edgar Lee. *The Tale of Chicago* (New York: Putnam's Sons, 1933), 189.

16. Wille, Lois. *Forever Open, Clear and Free – The Historic Struggle for Chicago's Lakefront* (Chicago: Henry Regnery Company, 1972), 81.

17. Darby, Edwin. *The Fortune Builders. Garden City* (New York: Doubleday & Company, Inc., 1986), 168.

18. Ross, Ishbel. *Silhouette In Diamonds – The Life of Mrs. Potter Palmer* (New York: Harper & Brothers, Publishers, 1960), 47.

19. Ross, Ishbel. *Silhouette In Diamonds – The Life of Mrs. Potter Palmer* (New York: Harper & Brothers, Publishers, 1960), 44.

20. Per conversation with Pauline Wood Egan, July 2002.

21. Miller, Donald L. *City of the Century: The Epic of Chicago and the Making of America* (New York: Simon & Schuster, 1996), 416.

22. Beveridge, Albert J. III and Radomsky, Susan. *An American Girl Travels Into the Twentieth Century – The Chronicles of Catherine Eddy Beveridge* (Lanham, MD: Hamilton Books, 2005), 112–113.

CHAPTER 2

1. Wille, Lois. *Forever Open, Clear and Free – The Historic Struggle for Chicago's Lakefront* (Chicago: Henry Regnery Company, 1972), 57.

2. Poole, Ernest. *Giants Gone – Men Who Made Chicago* (New York: McGraw-Hill Book Company, 1943), 109.

3. Meeker, Arthur. *Chicago, With Love – A Polite and Personal History* (New York: Alfred A. Knopf, 1955), 33.

4. Stamper, John W. *Chicago's North Michigan Avenue – Planning and Development 1900–1930* (Chicago: The University of Chicago Press, 1991), 4.

5. Meeker, Arthur. *Chicago, With Love – A Polite and Personal History* (New York: Alfred A. Knopf, 1955), 31.

6. Stamper, John W. *Chicago's North Michigan Avenue – Planning and Development 1900–1930* (Chicago: The University of Chicago Press, 1991), 14–19.

CHAPTER 3

1. Ross, Ishbel. *Silhouette In Diamonds – The Life of Mrs. Potter Palmer* (New York: Harper & Brothers, Publishers, 1960), 52.

2. Ross, Ishbel. *Silhouette In Diamonds – The Life of Mrs. Potter Palmer* (New York: Harper & Brothers, Publishers, 1960), 55.

3. Ross, Ishbel. *Silhouette In Diamonds – The Life of Mrs. Potter Palmer* (New York: Harper & Brothers, Publishers, 1960), 53.

4. Francis Webber Sever, Harvard graduate, wrote his aunt in a letter from the Columbian Exposition. First letter, no date.

5. Tallmadge, Thomas E. *Architecture In Old Chicago.* (Chicago: The University of Chicago Press, 1941), 185.

6. Erens, Patricia. *Masterpieces, Famous Chicagoans and Their Paintings* (Chicago: Chicago Review Press, 1979), 29.

7. Miller, Donald L. *City of the Century: The Epic of Chicago and the Making of America* (New York: Simon & Schuster, 1996), 414.

8. Ross, Ishbel. *Silhouette In Diamonds – The Life of Mrs. Potter Palmer* (New York: Harper & Brothers, Publishers, 1960), 38.

9. Kansas City Star Newspaper, May 6, 1918.

10. Weimann, Jeanne Madeline. *The Fair Women – The Story of The Woman's Building World's Columbian Exposition Chicago 1893* (Chicago: Academy Chicago, 1981), 560.

11. Beadle, Muriel. *The Fortnightly of Chicago The City and Its Women: 1873–1973* (Chicago: Henry Regnery Co., 1973), 9.

12. Miller, Donald L. *City of the Century: The Epic of Chicago and the Making of America* (New York: Simon & Schuster, 1996), 416.

13. Weimann, Jeanne Madeline. *The Fair Women – The Story of The Woman's Building World's Columbian Exposition Chicago 1893* (Chicago: Academy Chicago, 1981), 17.

14. Tallmadge, Thomas E. *Architecture In Old Chicago.* (Chicago: The University of Chicago Press, 1941), 142.

15. Miller, Donald L. *City of the Century: The Epic of Chicago and the Making of America* (New York: Simon & Schuster, 1996), 415.

16. Furer, Howard B., ed. *Chicago: A Chronological & Documentary History, 1784–1970* (Dobbs Ferry, NY: Oceana Publications, 1974), 25.

CHAPTER 4

1. Mayer, Harold M. and Wade, Richard C. *Chicago – Growth of a Metropolis* (Chicago: The University of Chicago Press, 1969), 151.

2. Poole, Ernest. *Giants Gone – Men Who Made Chicago* (New York: McGraw-Hill Book Company, 1943), 195.

3. Wille, Lois. *Forever Open, Clear and Free – The Historic Struggle for Chicago's Lakefront* (Chicago: Henry Regnery Company, 1972), 40.

4. Bowen, Louise de Koven. *Growing Up With A City* (Urbana and Chicago: University of Illinois Press, 2002), 22.

5. Bowen, Louise de Koven. *Growing Up With A City* (Urbana and Chicago: University of Illinois Press, 2002), 21-22.

6. Wille, Lois. *Forever Open, Clear and Free – The Historic Struggle for Chicago's Lakefront* (Chicago: Henry Regnery Company, 1972), 41.

7. Lewis, Lloyd and Smith, Henry Justin. *Chicago, The History of Its Reputation* (New York: Harcourt, Brace and Company, 1929), 190.

8. Miller, Donald L. *City of the Century: The Epic of Chicago and the Making of America* (New York: Simon & Schuster, 1996), 309.

9. Harrison, Mrs. Carter H. *"Strange To Say" Recollections of Persons and Events in New Orleans and Chicago* (Chicago: A. Kroch and Son Publishers, 1949), 76.

10. Bowen, Louise de Koven. *Growing Up With A City* (Urbana and Chicago: University of Illinois Press, 2002), 150.

11. Longstreth, Richard, ed. *The Charnley House: Louis Sullivan, Frank Lloyd Wright, and the Making of Chicago's Gold Coast* (Chicago: The University of Chicago Press, 2004), 51.

12. Miller, Donald L. *City of the Century: The Epic of Chicago and the Making of America* (New York: Simon & Schuster, 1996), 331.

13. Miller, Donald L. *City of the Century: The Epic of Chicago and the Making of America* (New York: Simon & Schuster, 1996), 316.

14. Poole, Ernest. *Giants Gone – Men Who Made Chicago* (New York: McGraw-Hill Book Company, 1943), 184.

15. Burg, David F. *Chicago's White City of 1893* (Lexington: The University Press of Kentucky, 1976), 119.

16. Weimann, Jeanne Madeline. *The Fair Women – The Story of The Woman's Building World's Columbian Exposition Chicago 1893* (Chicago: Academy Chicago, 1981), 218.

17. Williams, Ellen. "Harriet Monroe and 'Poetry' Magazine." *Chicago History, Winter 1975–1976* (1976): 206.

CHAPTER 5

1. Gregory, Addie Hibbard. *A GreatGrandmother Remembers* (Chicago: Kroch and Son, 1941), 82.

2. Faulkner, Joseph W. "Painters at the Hall of Expositions: 1890." *Chicago History, Spring 1972* (1972): 16.

3. Harris, Neil. *Chicago's Dream, A World's Treasure: The Art Institute of Chicago 1893–1993* (Chicago: The Art Institute of Chicago, 1993), 35.

4. Gregory, Addie Hibbard. *A GreatGrandmother Remembers* (Chicago: Kroch and Son, 1941), 161.

5. Gregory, Addie Hibbard. *A GreatGrandmother Remembers* (Chicago: Kroch and Son, 1941), 157.

6. Saarinen, Aline B. *The Proud Possessors – The Lives, Times and Tastes of Some Adventurous American Art Collectors* (New York: Random House, 1958), 20.

7. Brettell, Richard R. "Monet's Haystacks Reconsidered." *The Art Institute of Chicago Museum Studies, Volume 11, No. 1 Fall 1984* (1984): 19.

8. Ross, Ishbel. *Silhouette In Diamonds – The Life of Mrs. Potter Palmer* (New York: Harper & Brothers, Publishers, 1960), 155.

9. Ross, Ishbel. *Silhouette In Diamonds – The Life of Mrs. Potter Palmer* (New York: Harper & Brothers, Publishers, 1960), 155.

10. Brettell, Richard R. "Monet's Haystacks Reconsidered." *The Art Institute of Chicago Museum Studies, Volume 11, No. 1 Fall 1984* (1984): 6, 19-20.

11. Mathews, Nancy Mowll. *Mary Cassatt – A Life* (New Haven: Yale University Press, 1994), 203.

12. Mathews, Nancy Mowll. *Mary Cassatt – A Life* (New Haven: Yale University Press, 1994), 217.

13. Mathews, Nancy Mowll. *Mary Cassatt – A Life* (New Haven: Yale University Press, 1994), 204.

14. Webster, Sally. *Eve's Daughter/Modern Woman – A Mural of Mary Cassatt.* (Urbana: The University of Illinois Press, 2004), 100-101.

15. Mathews, Nancy Mowll. *Mary Cassatt – A Life* (New Haven: Yale University Press, 1994), 213.

16. Andrews, Wayne. *Battle For Chicago* (New York: Harcourt, Brace and Company, 1946), 150.

17. Erens, Patricia. *Masterpieces, Famous Chicagoans and Their Paintings* (Chicago: Chicago Review Press, 1979), 21.

18. Saarinen, Aline B. *The Proud Possessors – The Lives, Times and Tastes of Some Adventurous American Art Collectors* (New York: Random House, 1958), 13.

19. Weimann, Jeanne Madeline. *The Fair Women – The Story of The Woman's Building World's Columbian Exposition Chicago 1893* (Chicago: Academy Chicago, 1981), 322.

20. Saarinen, Aline B. *The Proud Possessors – The Lives, Times and Tastes of Some Adventurous American Art Collectors* (New York: Random House, 1958), 15.

21. Ross, Ishbel. *Silhouette In Diamonds – The Life of Mrs. Potter Palmer* (New York: Harper & Brothers, Publishers, 1960), 100.

CHAPTER 6

1. Weimann, Jeanne Madeline. *The Fair Women – The Story of The Woman's Building World's Columbian Exposition Chicago 1893* (Chicago: Academy Chicago, 1981), 215.

2. Wille, Lois. *Forever Open, Clear and Free – The Historic Struggle for Chicago's Lakefront* (Chicago: Henry Regnery Company, 1972), 64.

3. Miller, Donald L. *City of the Century: The Epic of Chicago and the Making of America* (New York: Simon & Schuster, 1996), 379.

4. Darby, Edwin. *The Fortune Builders. Garden City* (New York: Doubleday & Company, Inc., 1986), 42.

5. Andrews, Wayne. *Battle For Chicago* (New York: Harcourt, Brace and Company, 1946), 147.

6. Hirsch, Susan E. and Goler, Robert I. *A City Comes of Age: Chicago in the 1890s* (Chicago: Chicago Historical Society, 1990), 47.

7. Hirsch, Susan E. and Goler, Robert I. *A City Comes of Age: Chicago in the 1890s* (Chicago: Chicago Historical Society, 1990), 24.

8. Miller, Donald L. *City of the Century: The Epic of Chicago and the Making of America* (New York: Simon & Schuster, 1996), 505.

9. Miller, Donald L. *City of the Century: The Epic of Chicago and the Making of America* (New York: Simon & Schuster, 1996), 382.

10. Smith, Henry Justin. *Chicago A Portrait* (New York: The Century Co., 1931), 181.

11. Burg, David F. *Chicago's White City of 1893* (Lexington: The University Press of Kentucky, 1976), 79.

12. Poole, Ernest. *Giants Gone – Men Who Made Chicago* (New York: McGraw-Hill Book Company, 1943), 174.

13. Longstreet, Stephen. *Chicago 1860–1919* (New York: David McKay Company, Inc., 1973), 274.

14. Poole, Ernest. *Giants Gone – Men Who Made Chicago* (New York: McGraw-Hill Book Company, 1943), 168.

15. Burg, David F. *Chicago's White City of 1893* (Lexington: The University Press of Kentucky, 1976), 99.

16. Burg, David F. *Chicago's White City of 1893* (Lexington: The University Press of Kentucky, 1976), 304.

17. Burg, David F. *Chicago's White City of 1893* (Lexington: The University Press of Kentucky, 1976), 299.

18. Poole, Ernest. *Giants Gone – Men Who Made Chicago* (New York: McGraw-Hill Book Company, 1943), 189.

19. Gregory, Addie Hibbard. *A GreatGrandmother Remembers* (Chicago: Kroch and Son, 1941), 148.

20. Bushnell, George. "Out Of the Ordinary; Once Bicycles Shifted From High-Wheeled Monsters, They Ruled Chicago Roads." *The Chicago Tribune, January 2, 2005* (2005), 5.

21. Bushnell, George. "Out Of the Ordinary; Once Bicycles Shifted From High-Wheeled Monsters, They Ruled Chicago Roads." *The Chicago Tribune, January 2, 2005* (2005), 5.

22. Weimann, Jeanne Madeline. "A Temple to Women's Genius: The Woman's Building of 1893." *Chicago History, Spring 1977* (1977): 23.

23. Weimann, Jeanne Madeline. "A Temple to Women's Genius: The Woman's Building of 1893." *Chicago History, Spring 1977* (1977): 25.

24. Weimann, Jeanne Madeline. "A Temple to Women's Genius: The Woman's Building of 1893." *Chicago History, Spring 1977* (1977): 32.

25. Webster, Sally. *Eve's Daughter/Modern Woman – A Mural of Mary Cassatt.* (Urbana: The University of Illinois Press, 2004), 52.

26. Weimann, Jeanne Madeline. *The Fair Women – The Story of The Woman's Building World's Columbian Exposition Chicago 1893* (Chicago: Academy Chicago, 1981), 430–432.

27. Weimann, Jeanne Madeline. *The Fair Women – The Story of The Woman's Building World's Columbian Exposition Chicago 1893* (Chicago: Academy Chicago, 1981), 175.

28. Weimann, Jeanne Madeline. *The Fair Women – The Story of The Woman's Building World's Columbian Exposition Chicago 1893* (Chicago: Academy Chicago, 1981), 79-80.

29. Weimann, Jeanne Madeline. *The Fair Women – The Story of The Woman's Building World's Columbian Exposition Chicago 1893* (Chicago: Academy Chicago, 1981), 267.

30. Burg, David F. *Chicago's White City of 1893* (Lexington: The University Press of Kentucky, 1976), 224.

31. Harrison, Mrs. Carter H. *"Strange To Say" Recollections of Persons and Events in New Orleans and Chicago* (Chicago: A. Kroch and Son Publishers, 1949), 66.

32. Gregory, Addie Hibbard. *A GreatGrandmother Remembers* (Chicago: Kroch and Son, 1941), 148.

33. Longstreet, Stephen. *Chicago 1860–1919* (New York: David McKay Company, Inc., 1973), 288.

34. Shaw, Marian. *World's Fair Notes – A Woman Journalist Views Chicago's 1893 Columbian Exposition* (Pogo Press, 1992), 64.

35. Weimann, Jeanne Madeline. *The Fair Women – The Story of The Woman's Building World's Columbian Exposition Chicago 1893* (Chicago: Academy Chicago, 1981), 582.

CHAPTER 7

1. Ross, Ishbel. *Silhouette In Diamonds – The Life of Mrs. Potter Palmer* (New York: Harper & Brothers, Publishers, 1960), 121

2. Erens, Patricia. *Masterpieces, Famous Chicagoans and Their Paintings* (Chicago: Chicago Review Press, 1979), 31.

3. Harris, Neil. *Chicago's Dream, A World's Treasure: The Art Institute of Chicago 1893–1993* (Chicago: The Art Institute of Chicago, 1993), 31.

4. Saarinen, Aline B. *The Proud Possessors – The Lives, Times and Tastes of Some Adventurous American Art Collectors* (New York: Random House, 1958), 6.

5. Weimann, Jeanne Madeline. *The Fair Women – The Story of The Woman's Building World's Columbian Exposition Chicago 1893* (Chicago: Academy Chicago, 1981), 219.

BIBLIOGRAPHY

Andrews, Wayne. *A Social History of American Architecture: Architecture, Ambition and Americans*. New York: The Free Press, 1969.

Andrews, Wayne. *Battle For Chicago*. New York: Harcourt, Brace and Company, 1946.

Appelbaum, Stanley. *The Chicago World's Fair of 1893 – A Photographic Record*. New York: Dover Publications, 1980.

Art Institute of Chicago, Museum Studies, Volume 28, Number 2. *Gifts Beyond Measure: The Antiquarian Society and European Decorative Arts, 1987–2002*. Chicago: The Art Institute of Chicago, 2002.

Beadle, Muriel. *The Fortnightly of Chicago The City and Its Women: 1873–1973*. Chicago: Henry Regnery Co., 1973.

Beveridge, Albert J. III and Radomsky, Susan. *An American Girl Travels Into the Twentieth Century – The Chronicles of Catherine Eddy Beveridge*. Lanham, MD: Hamilton Books, 2005.

Bowen, Louise de Koven. *Growing Up With A City*. Urbana and Chicago: University of Illinois Press, 2002.

Brettell, Richard R. "Monet's Haystacks Reconsidered." *The Art Institute of Chicago Museum Studies, Volume 11, No. 1 Fall 1984* (1984): 4-21.

Burg, David F. *Chicago's White City of 1893*. Lexington: The University Press of Kentucky, 1976.

Bushnell, George. *Out Of the Ordinary; Once Bicycles Shifted From HighWheeled Monsters, They Ruled Chicago Roads*. Chicago: The Chicago Tribune, January 2, 2005.

Cromie, Robert. *A Short History of Chicago*. San Francisco, Lexikos, 1984.

Darby, Edwin. *The Fortune Builders*. Garden City, New York: Doubleday & Company, Inc., 1986.

Drury, John. *Old Chicago Houses*. Chicago: The University of Chicago Press, 1941.

Erens, Patricia. *Masterpieces, Famous Chicagoans and Their Paintings*. Chicago: Chicago Review Press, 1979.

Faulkner, Joseph W. "Painters at the Hall of Expositions: 1890." *Chicago History, Spring 1972* (1972): 14–17.

Furer, Howard B., ed. *Chicago: A Chronological & Documentary History, 1784–1970*. Dobbs Ferry, NY: Oceana Publications, 1974.

Grant, Bruce. *Fight For A City: The Story of the Union League Club of Chicago and Its Times, 1880–1955*. Chicago: Rand McNally & Company, 1955.

Gregory, Addie Hibbard. *A GreatGrandmother Remembers*. Chicago: Kroch and Son, 1941.

Harris, Neil. *Chicago's Dream, A World's Treasure: The Art Institute of Chicago 1893–1993*. Chicago: The Art Institute of Chicago, 1993.

Harrison, Carter H. *Growing Up With Chicago, Sequel to "Story Years"*. Chicago: Ralph Fletcher Seymour, 1944.

Harrison, Carter H. *Stormy Years: The Autobiography of Carter H. Harrison Five Times Mayor of Chicago*. Indianapolis: Bobbs-Merrill Company, 1935.

Harrison, Mrs. Carter H. *"Strange To Say" Recollections of Persons and Events in New Orleans and Chicago.* Chicago: A. Kroch and Son Publishers, 1949.

Hirsch, Susan E. and Goler, Robert I. *A City Comes of Age: Chicago in the 1890s.* Chicago: Chicago Historical Society, 1990.

Hoffman, Donald. *The Architecture of John Wellborn Root.* Chicago: The University of Chicago Press, 1973.

Kogan, Herman. *Seeman's Historic Cities Series, No. 22. Yesterday's Chicago.* Miami: E. A. Seeman Publishing, Inc.

Lewis, Lloyd and Smith, Henry Justin. *Chicago, The History of Its Reputation.* New York: Harcourt, Brace and Company, 1929.

Longstreet, Stephen. *Chicago 1860–1919.* New York: David McKay Company, Inc., 1973.

Longstreth, Richard, ed. *The Charnley House: Louis Sullivan, Frank Lloyd Wright, and the Making of Chicago's Gold Coast.* Chicago: The University of Chicago Press, 2004.

Lowe, David Garrard. *Chicago Interiors: Views of A Splendid World.* New York: Wing Books, 1979.

Lowe, David Garrard. *Lost Chicago.* New York: Watson-Guptill, 2000.

Martin, Ralph G. *Cissy: The Extraordinary Life of Eleanor Medill Patterson.* New York: Simon & Schuster, 1979.

Masters, Edgar Lee. *The Tale of Chicago.* New York: Putnam's Sons, 1933.

Mathews, Nancy Mowll. *Mary Cassatt – A Life.* New Haven: Yale University Press, 1994.

Mayer, Harold M. and Wade, Richard C. *Chicago – Growth of a Metropolis.* Chicago: The University of Chicago Press, 1969.

Meeker, Arthur. *Chicago, With Love – A Polite and Personal History.* New York: Alfred A. Knopf, 1955.

Miller, Donald L. *City of the Century: The Epic of Chicago and the Making of America.* New York: Simon & Schuster, 1996.

Poole, Ernest. *Giants Gone – Men Who Made Chicago.* New York: McGraw-Hill Book Company, 1943.

Ross, Ishbel. *Silhouette In Diamonds – The Life of Mrs. Potter Palmer.* New York: Harper & Brothers, Publishers, 1960.

Saarinen, Aline B. *The Proud Possessors – The Lives, Times and Tastes of Some Adventurous American Art Collectors.* New York: Random House, 1958.

Shaw, Marian. *World's Fair Notes – A Woman Journalist Views Chicago's 1893 Columbian Exposition.* Pogo Press, 1992.

Shepp, James W. and Shepp, Daniel B. *Shepp's World's Fair Photographed.* Chicago: Globe Bible Publishing Co., 1983.

Smith, Henry Justin. *Chicago A Portrait.* New York: The Century Co., 1931.

Stamper, John W. *Chicago's North Michigan Avenue – Planning and Development 1900–1930.* Chicago: The University of Chicago Press, 1991.

Tallmadge, Thomas E. *Architecture In Old Chicago.* Chicago: The University of Chicago Press, 1941.

Webster, Sally. *Eve's Daughter/Modern Woman – A Mural of Mary Cassatt.* Urbana: The University of Illinois Press, 2004.

Weimann, Jeanne Madeline. "A Temple to Women's Genius: The Woman's Building of 1893." *Chicago History, Spring 1977* (1977): 23–33.

Weimann, Jeanne Madeline. *The Fair Women – The Story of The Woman's Building World's Columbian Exposition Chicago 1893.* Chicago: Academy Chicago, 1981.

Wille, Lois. *Forever Open, Clear and Free – The Historic Struggle for Chicago's Lakefront.* Chicago: Henry Regnery Company, 1972.

Williams, Ellen. "Harriet Monroe and 'Poetry' Magazine." *Chicago History, Winter 1975–1976* (1976): 204–212.

Zorbaugh, Harvey Warren. *The Gold Coast and the Slum – A Sociological Study of Chicago's Near North Side.* Chicago: The University of Chicago Press: 1929.